Fractured Motherhood

Maggie Walters

Blue Gum Publishing

First published in Australia in 2026 by Blue Gum Publishing.

Blue Gum Publishing acknowledges the Traditional Owners and their custodianship of the lands on which this book was written, the Widjabul Wia-bal people of the Bundjalung Nation, who are the original storytellers of this region. We pay our respects to their Ancestors and their descendants, who continue cultural and spiritual connections to Country.

FRACTURED MOTHERHOOD

ISBN: 978-0-6486038-3-2

A catalogue record for this work is available from the National Library of Australia

Cover design: Hazel Lam

This book is dedicated to my children.
There are no words to express the depth and breadth
of love I have for each of you.
You are my joy and my light.

WARNING:

Readers should be aware that parts of this book describe childhood violence, trauma, and suicidality. Please take care of yourself and ensure your own emotional safety when reading.

Contents

Fractured Motherhood

A Word Before

When I began, I intended this story to be a love letter to my children, about adoption and how we came to be a family. It was supposed to be a story about the fulfilment of my dream to be a mother and the not-so-linear story that brought us together.

I was equally determined this would not be a story of living with Dissociative Identity Disorder (DID) or Multiple Personality Disorder (MPD), as it was known at the time of my diagnosis. I detail all of this in my first book, *SPLIT*, where I discuss coming to terms with my diagnosis and the physical and sexual abuse I experienced at the hands of the Parents, learning to live with the creative and quirky way my young, malleable mind developed to cope with the trauma. In *Fractured Motherhood*, my intention instead was to tell a story about the beauty of our family's origins, leaving my trauma behind. I mean really, what did my mental health have to do with raising kids?

I wanted to write something beautiful. Devoid of trauma.

I was naïve.

It often happens with writers; we start with one concept, but it inevitably morphs and takes on a life of its own. This happened to me. I began this love letter to my kids, creating wonder and intimacy in words to reflect our journey to each other.

Honestly? It was sickly sweet. It needed more guts and conflict. Apart from acknowledging our struggles—and often, despair—as we fought to navigate our way through the bureaucratic labyrinth of international adoption, I was whitewashing the specific challenges I faced, normalising my fears of parenting to the point of avoiding the truth of my history. I was sidestepping an examination of the underlying reasons for my own personal angst about motherhood.

Practically speaking, it also became clear that readers who did not already know me through *SPLIT* would only get half the story. *SPLIT* gives the reader an intimate look inside my head, revealing how my system of *alters* permeates every aspect of my life. But this story, without the open disclosure that I am someone who lives with MPD, was not painting an accurate picture of who I was as a mother. By refusing to acknowledge my history as part of our adoption journey, I was denying the truth of my life, which in *SPLIT* I had worked so hard to acknowledge.

I sat down again, fleshing out a more realistic story—one that was more than a love story to my children. I wanted to shine a light, not only on the delight my children bring me but also to be honest about the struggles of parenting, which confront someone with mental health challenges. Without this, my story of our family was incomplete and shallow.

> Dissociative Identity Disorder (DID), previously known as Multiple Personality Disorder, is a mental health condition where an individual experiences two or more distinct identities or personality states, which recurrently take control of their behaviour. It is characterised by a disconnection from one's thoughts, memories, feelings, and sense of self, and often involves significant memory gaps. This condition is typically linked to severe trauma experienced during childhood. (Source: Cleveland Clinic)

While the mental health community calls MPD a mental health condition, I have grown to see it as something more. It is a creative tool for coping with horrific abuse. When I think about how and why I came to have MPD, I realise it is a pretty astounding survival mechanism.

MPD occurs almost exclusively in those who have suffered extreme trauma as a child because it is the young brain which has the plasticity to adapt to the trauma and survive. In my case, I was three when I experienced the trauma which was the catalyst for my MPD. From then until the age of almost 16, I was sexually abused by the Parents and groomed for use in a paedophile ring through contacts of my Father. In order to survive this abuse, my mind adapted; it split. This action protected me from the trauma of the abuse. Unique identities or alters instead suffered the abuse inflicted on my body, while I hid my consciousness away in the recesses of my mind. I call my alters, *The Girls*.

Everyone who is multiple has a system—an internal thread bringing order to the chaos of having these multiple personalities. For some, a single internal alter controls most of the others, acting as a manager to minimise possible chaos. This is what happened for me. My family emigrated to the United States from England when I was three, and it was on the ship crossing the Atlantic where I first experienced the trauma which caused me to mentally disappear. I gave way, and *Annie* became. She remains my system administrator.

During our childhood and young adult years, my consciousness stayed hidden away, dormant. It was *Annie* who lived and managed our multiple life. Her role was to organise the external day-to-day routine and the 'job' allocated to each alter, who *Annie* (and now I) refer to as *The Girls*. Each 'job' was specific to one of *The Girls*—when they were confronted with an abusive situation, it was that *Girl's* job to emerge and endure the specific trauma.

Another creative aspect of bringing order to the chaos was the organisation of the system around a house, where each of *The Girls* has her own room or space, either inside, or sometimes outside, the house. This is where *The Girls* exist, and from where they emerged to do their job, bringing a sense of stability to what was otherwise a chaotic life.

Although the sexual abuse ended by the time *Annie* was 16, I (Maggie) didn't reemerge until *Annie* was in her early 30s. (This is discussed thoroughly in *SPLIT*.) So, although I am now consciously Maggie, *Annie* and *The Girls* are still a part of my existence, living in my mind as distinct individual identities.

I would love to say I always get along with *Annie* and *The Girls*, but that isn't the case. Although I acknowledge the role they played in allowing me to survive my childhood abuse, we often disagree about how I live my life now. We are a dysfunctional family; the difference being my family lives in my mind. It's never quiet. I hear their day-to-day chatter and feel the emotions they carry from a lifetime of pain. There are any number of things in my daily routine which *Annie* and *The Girls* experience as a threat. I can, sometimes, block out their responses, but they are always with me, providing me with their unique perspectives on how I navigate my life.

What does this mean in relation to my story? Being asleep for all those years meant I was relieved of experiencing the abuse which *The Girls* suffered on my behalf. Even today, I only learn about memories from my childhood if *The Girls* choose to share them with me.

Stories in this book of our childhood and young adult life are from *Annie's* perspective. In *SPLIT*, I was specific about identifying which sections were written by other alters. For this memoir, I have been more general in my approach because this is primarily a story about motherhood. *Annie's* existence revolved around the woman who was Mother. She was in effect, *Annie's* mother. *Annie*'s stories are her experience of surviving as a child and then, as a young adult, coming to terms with who she was.

Contrary to the stereotype projected in the media, people who are multiple rarely present as chaotic or, dare I say, psychotic. This isn't the norm and certainly doesn't apply to my life. Unless something triggers me, you would never know I was multiple. And even on those odd occasions when one of *The Girls* emerges with her response to a situation, a bystander would suspect nothing. At best, they might assume I was emotionally out of sorts.

I am open about living with MPD and discussing how our system works. I do this both to help reduce the many stigmas around complex mental health issues, but also to acknowledge the debt I owe to my young mind, which had the adaptive plasticity to help me endure my childhood. *The Girls,* in truth, are my superheroes. They lived through a life of trauma and predatory exploitation so I could survive. I owe them my life.

In this book, all the names I use are pseudonyms, including my system of alters. Some *Girls* I refer to by a title which projects the essence of who they are. For instance, *Angry Girl*'s job is, simply, to be angry. Understandably, each alter, in their individual way, felt great anger at the abuse they suffered. It is still *Angry Girl*'s role to hold anger so others could survive. *Angry Girl* is not her real name, but this pseudonym paints an accurate picture of who she is.

What I have described would be difficult for a neurotypical reader to understand. But I ask you to accept that, for me, as I live with my multiplicity, it is indeed logical for *Annie* to be a complete, separate individual living in my mind and was the presenting personality for our childhood and the bulk of our young adult life. She lived through it all and was privy to all the ugliness and pain. *Annie*'s life is at the heart of this story. This is especially true of *Annie*'s relationship with Mother. It was *Annie* who had a relationship with Mother in our childhood, and it is now me who must account for the consequences of that relationship. For obvious reasons, this is relevant in the issues I now face as a mother myself.

It is also important to note how *Annie* tells her story. We have an alter named *Writer*, whose job is to tell *Annie* and *The Girls'* stories, in their voice and on their behalf. The stories in this book are told with *Annie's* approval. They are, after all, *Annie's* stories to tell.

These days, *Annie* sits in the front window of the house, which is *The Girls'* home in my head. *Annie* would tell you, in her own words, *I am not Maggie. If you are going to read this story and understand what parenting has been like for her, then you have to understand my life. I lived our childhood while Maggie lives with the ramifications of our history. So, what I ask, all I ask, is for you to remember that the stories or flashbacks about our childhood belong to* The Girls *and me. We are separate and unique. If the point of this story is about parenting with mental health challenges, then it is important you remember our system—me and* The Girls*—we are the mental health challenge Maggie faces.*

I wonder at times what you, the reader, is thinking when we write about my life as a child. When I talk about my emotions and experiences, are you able to allow me my identity as an individual? Or do you see me as some sort of vague alter-ego of Maggie? Can you accept I have my own feelings, thoughts and desires which exist separately from Maggie's? This is how I wish you to read this story. I am not Maggie, or a version of Maggie. I am Annie.

The idea of a shared narrative—or shared life—is something people who are not MPD often find difficult to understand. I'm asking (or perhaps *we* are asking) you to take a risk and accept there are two narrators telling the story, and they offer different perspectives on our shared life experiences.

CRACKS EXPOSED

Tapestry

I see my therapist every week, artfully navigating around the topic of Mother, talking around the edges of who she was. It's how I approach trauma memories or triggers, skirting around the matter rather than talking directly to the issue at hand. I easily go into fight-or-flight mode if I feel too confronted. So, this gentle approach seems logical. It's safe and gives me control as I find a way to be honest about what is going on in my head. Trust was (and is) a huge issue for me.

I often get frustrated with myself because I've been seeing this therapist (my fourth shrink!) for almost a decade now, and trust remains a central issue for me. It's not him. He's actually a gentle soul. It's me—it's *The Girls*. A lifetime of betrayal makes trust almost impossible. I don't trust the process. I fear what might be uncovered if I completely let my guard down, if I allowed the indiscriminate mess in my head about Mother to come gushing out. What would it look like? Do I trust my therapist to help me keep it all corralled and manageable? I doubt it. Do I trust myself to cope and wrestle with it? Definitely not.

I remember one day when I was feeling highly anxious as I left for my weekly date with my shrink. I knew something was amiss because I had downed Panadol for a headache and spent half the morning on the toilet. The other kicker was my jaw was locking up. This had been happening more as I began working through issues around Mother. I was painfully aware that these were my telltale signs something was going on in the recesses of my brain with *The Girls.* It needed to be addressed.

My therapist gave me the normal methods with which to cope: clench fists, curl toes, breathe deeply. And then he stopped himself.

'You don't like that sort of work to control your anxiety. I'll stop now.'

And he was right—to a point. I appreciated the techniques, often doing them at home, knowing they kept me grounded. I simply didn't want to do it in front of him. It was embarrassing. Exposing. It required trust. I absolutely believed taking part in this sort of therapeutic exercise would calm me. But I also believed my armour of dissociation and anxiety would melt away. I might not be so reticent about looking at the dark shadows behind my constant denial.

Would I get clarity?

What if? What if I could see past the veneer of self-protection and talk about those dark shadows I didn't understand? What if I listened to *The Girls*, these voices, wrestling with the things they knew about our childhood and were prepared to talk about, bringing perspective to who we were?

What if they talked about Mother? Instead of lurking around the edges of my relationship with her, what if we talked directly to the matter? What if I untangled the rough edges of a patchy tapestry of memories, which frequently seemed illogical? What would *The Girls* share? What would I see? Feel? Fear?

More importantly, would it destroy me?

It terrifies me to look at the litany of what I remember of Mother. Living with limited images and memories is uncomfortable, but safe and manageable. I was a fat, ugly child and an utter disappointment. I was an academic failure and made her look bad. All I ever craved was her love. But it seemed to go wanting. I could do nothing to earn her love. These are the ironic things I like to believe I can wrestle with—the things I already comprehend, my security blanket. The things I know intimately are more comforting than the fear of the unknown. If I looked closer, allowed *The Girls* to process their pain, would I be affected?

I was quietly being bombarded again and again with the same questions. *The Girls* were constantly at a loss to understand how Mother could stand by, groom me even, for the world Father and his friends used me for. What made her the sort of person who would turn a blind eye to her child's abuse? This question terrified me. What happened to the young woman I see in pictures? What circumstances in her life compelled her to acquiesce? Fearfully, I consider—am I destined for the same?

A Mother's Touch

As a small child, Mother would wash my hair in the kitchen sink. I was three, maybe four, and she would drag a chair over from the kitchen table and get me to stand on it. When I was older, she taught me to bring the chair over myself. I loved those moments, feeling like I was a grown up. She would pat the back of the chair and smile, telling me to *pop up to the sink*. I would wear just my undies, which was a pragmatic decision to ensure my clothes didn't get wet.

Eagerly climbing up, I leaned into the feeling of being near Mother, waiting with excitement while she brought a towel and shampoo to the kitchen. I would put my hands on the edge of the counter, feeling the slick surface of the sink. All the dishes had been done and put away; the basin was clean and ready for action.

From my raised perch, I could see through a set of half-sized folding screens, always open. It was fun to peer through this space. Often Father would be there, sitting in his chair, reading a journal, savouring a glass of rum or whisky, whatever he had on hand.

Bits and bobs from Mother's painting paraphernalia often cluttered the windowsill. Brushes in tins, waiting to be used, or piles of magazines she scoured to find the latest masterpiece she intended to interpret. Painting was her hobby and passion. I was proud Mother was such a talented artist. A ceramic blue wren sat on the windowsill. It seemed forlorn and alone; I sometimes wondered what it would sound like if it sang bird tunes. It was silly to give animated thoughts to a piece of decorative clay, but these are the things a child's mind does while waiting patiently for grown-ups.

There was no need for words; I knew the routine well. Mother would hand me a small towel that I scrunched around my neck, holding it tight to keep water from dripping down my body as she rinsed my hair.

She would pull the hose out of its slot. Her hands nuzzled my head down, beginning to soak my thick head of hair. Sometimes I heard her muttering to herself when she came across the thick knots I never seemed to keep at bay. These brief encounters would strike fear, and I would wonder how she would react to my inability to keep my hair free of tangles. But I never lingered, focusing instead on the washing, feeling her massage my head while rubbing the shampoo through my hair. Rinse and repeat.

What took less than five minutes was an experience my child's mind and heart lingered in. I could feel her warmth next to me, a hairbreadth away. When she reached her hands around my head, I could feel the soft pillow of her breasts against my body. Bliss! Intimate and tactile contact with Mother soothing my soul.

All too soon, she would be done. With the towel wrapped around my head in a turban, I laughed and skipped away, basking in the warmth of Mother's love. These brief moments were a blanket over the other experiences I had (children are very forgiving). I lived in these moments for as long as possible, holding this tender love close for those days when affection could not be found.

Mother's mood often dictated how she treated me when she would call me over to sit on a stool and set about combing out my locks. Brushing my wet, drippy, thick mop was a counterbalance to the closeness and touch we shared when she washed my hair. If she was in a good mood, she would handle these moments with ease, sitting me on her painting stool in the living room, TV on in the background. She might say something to me, or not. She might have a drink, or not. But when there was a gentleness in her actions, I savoured it, holding this mother/daughter intimacy close to my heart.

There were other times when my intuition made me wary of this post-washing hair-combing routine. Perhaps Mother had been drinking, or she and Father had a fight. Fear would set in when she started commenting on my horrible hair. I had failed her again. When she grumbled, my body would seize, becoming rigid as I clutched the edges of the stool to keep my balance when I heard the muttering under her breath. I knew what was to come, and the best way to get through it was to be strong, stiff and motionless. I would feel the brush struggle to pull through my hair. If I accidentally moved my head because of a yank, a slap would follow. To keep my head still while she brushed out the knots, she would place her palm firmly on my scalp and push away while the brush raked through my locks. Sometimes the knots were such a tangled mess she would not only pull out the knot, but sizeable chunks of hair as well. When I started school, she cut my hair off, leaving me with a short, less cumbersome bob.

Academic Truths

I found school difficult. I was always hypervigilant, looking for some sort of threat to my perceived sense of security. This made learning difficult, I became easily distracted and unfocused. Mathematics was a particular challenge. The numbers were often a jumbled mess on the page; I felt stupid.

Mother never went to parent–teacher interviews, so her attendance this time confused me. Had the teacher been in touch with her and already discussed my inattentiveness in class? Not knowing the answer terrified and confused my eight-year-old mind.

My two worlds of home and school abruptly collided. When Mother and my teacher greeted each other with familiarity, I did not expect this; my mind began swirling and my hands were sweating.

I sat outside the conversation. They were talking about me, not to me. I daydreamed about being out on the playground. Thinking about the swings was better than this weird feeling of being in my classroom and, well, not being taught.

I heard words they said like 'lazy', 'distracted', and the ultimate, 'I know she can do better'.

I waited, not sure what to expect.

Mother didn't talk to me as we went out to the car. I had embarrassed her again. I knew it. She always went silent when I did not live up to some unspoken expectation. I knew I was not the child she wanted. As we got in the car, I received a thwack across the back of my head, followed by a grumble. This time, it wasn't just because I was ugly and fat—I was stupid as well. A dumb, fat, lazy child. The rest of the trip home passed in silence.

Mother used silence as a subtle control. When we got home, I went to my room while she made dinner. More silence. I grew up in the heyday of this newfangled thing called a TV dinner. Instant meals heated through in the oven. Tough, gristly meat, pasty gravy, slimy, limp vegetables and the only thing I could stand, the apple crumble glop, which always ended up burnt. But it was new, exciting and freed up Mother's time.

After dinner, she put her hands on her hips, eyes wide, nostrils flared. 'Follow me.'

I shuffled behind her, obedient and quiet. My brain spun, trying to figure out what was going on. She walked into my bedroom, pulling a set of flashcards from her apron pocket.

'Your teacher says you get distracted, you don't try hard, especially with maths. She may not know how to get the best out of you, but I do. Sit down.'

She pulled out my desk chair and sat down, pointing for me to sit at the end of my bed. 'I'm going to hold a card up, and each time you get one wrong, I will smack you. Do you understand me?'

I gave her a slow, confused nod.

'No!' she yelled. 'Do you understand?'

'Yes, Mommy, I understand!' I was terrified and sat up straight.

'We'll see.' She shuffled through the pack. 'Let's try one to get you started, shall we?'

I nodded again.

She held up a card. Multiplication. She sighed. '5 x 4 is...?'

Oh! I could do this! 'Twenty.'

'Fine.'

Another card. 4 x 4. Maybe it wouldn't be so bad after all! 'That's 16!'

'Yes.'

And then another. 6 x 7. My mind went fuzzy. I could feel the answer at the edge of my mind but couldn't see it.

'What's the answer?'

Nothing. My mind was in chaos. I couldn't think of anything.

'Answer me!'

'Umm...25?' It was a guess. She knew it. I knew it.

'No!' She put the cards down. 'Come here.'

'I'm sorry! I can do another one.'

'No. Come here.' Her voice was steady, calculated.

I stood up. She grabbed my hand and pulled me face down across her lap. I felt the cold air against my bottom as she pulled down my underwear. Thwack. Once, twice, three times. Each harder than the last. No words, simply piercing pain.

Time seemed to stand still. More mistakes. More punishment. Stupid. Embarrassed. Idiot. This was the litany of words I told myself to justify the punishment I was receiving. I was Mother's fiercest disappointment. Later, I crawled under my bedsheets, bewildered. My sore bottom forcing me to sleep on my side.

Bedtime Stories

During my childhood, somewhere around the age of 10, I contracted glandular fever. Teenagers called it the kissing disease. Giggles would ensue, the assumption being you were making out with someone and, well, wasn't that cool. I had no boyfriend. Instead, it was part of an ongoing problem I faced with sexually transmitted diseases (STDs) as a child. The abuse at home, at the hands of Father's friends, was the likely culprit. Let's just say I was sick—really sick. I suffered from constant fatigue and a low-grade fever. My head hurt, my throat was sore, and my body ached. The kicker was the swollen lymph glands the doctor identified.

Mother's irritation at my inability to stay healthy vanished when the doctor diagnosed me. Did I see a flash of pity crossed her face? The doctor said I needed to stay home for a month. Antibiotics, bed rest and fluids would heal me.

Mother grumbled as we left the doctor and climbed into the car. 'You're old enough to take care of yourself, right?' It was a blunt, direct statement. A sharp reminder of how she did not like to be bothered by my presence. This viral impediment requiring her to actually help me was the ultimate insult.

I shrugged my shoulders. 'Yeah. Guess so.'

'I can't take the time off work. You need to do this yourself. You're big enough. Do you understand?' Her voice had a controlled edge. I had thrown off her routine; I was an irritation she didn't want to deal with. I always sensed her frustration at my existence. It was something I was attuned to—anticipating her impending disapproval and trying to avoid it. I went into an instinctual and interpretive mode, desperately trying to decipher these unsettling moments, looking for a way to respond to the growing tension.

This time, as with many others, I chose the path of least resistance, responding obediently, that yes, I could take care of myself.

Mother drew in a deep breath and looked at me with pity, as if she suddenly realised she was an adult and I was a child.

'Sorry. You're sick.' The quiet between us was deafening. She was being kind in her own ill-fashioned way. I had no point of reference for this compassion. And then, after a brief silence, 'How about we stop at the bookstore? Would you like a book or two to give you something to do while you rest?'

My eyes lit up. Books! She never spent money on me unless absolutely necessary. I remembered getting a book of fairy tales for Christmas one year, but never anything out of the blue like this. Between fatigue and headache, I uttered the most heartfelt *thank you* I could muster.

As soon as we pulled into the bookstore parking lot, my energy levels increased. The bell chimed on the door as we walked in. The woman behind the counter looked up and smiled. 'Can I help you?'

Mother's attentive, caring facade kicked in. 'My daughter needs books to read while she is recovering from being sick.'

The woman behind the counter smiled at me. 'Ah, we have so much to choose from! I'm sure you'll find just the ticket in the older kids' section. Just along the back wall.'

I felt Mother's growing impatience as I wandered the aisles, my fingers running over titles of books I had heard of but never read. A boxed set of books caught my eye. It had fairy-tale creatures and four children ready for battle, with a big bright lion watching in the background. I ran my fingers over the title, *The Chronicles of Narnia*, pulling it out gently to read the back of the box: a fantasy story about brothers and sisters lost in a magical world with talking animals. Then I looked at the price. It was three times the cost of the other books. I was nervous. How dare I ask for this special treat? I was entranced and determined, hoping desperately she would let me have this precious treat.

I took it up to the counter and put it down gently, hopeful my mother would be okay with the cost. 'This is what I'd like. Please, Mom.'

Mother never questioned the price. Perhaps it was guilt on her part. It didn't matter to me; I held this amazing gift on my lap all the way home.

Over the next month, I immersed myself in the world of these four children and the mythical land of Narnia, full of creatures that talked, fears to be faced and challenges to conquer. The story enraptured me.

Mother would occasionally call me from work to check on me, asking if I was resting and drinking fluids, and how my reading was going. They were never long calls; mother–daughter intimacy was an uncomfortable ill-fitted experience for both of us.

I made an art of taking these rare moments of engagement to build an image of a mother who loved me. A woman who cared about and cherished her daughter. I sifted out the pain, those experiences I simply didn't want to look at, and deciphered these cryptic words as her way of telling me she loved me. I did this to survive, building a fairy-tale world where Mother's love rescued me.

Fat Choices

Somewhere along the way, I became an embarrassment to Mother because I was fat. I'd gone from the roly-poly cute toddler people smiled and laughed at, to a rotund blob by the time I started school. I was not beautiful. This made Mother grumble.

I noticed it the most when we went shopping. She walked quickly through the local department store, muttering as she headed straight for the little girls' rack for larger girls, which was tucked away in the back corner of the store. Even the store thought being fat was something to be ashamed of. I would scurry behind Mother, my pudgy legs trying to keep up. She would have a quick look at the clothes, flicking through the hangers on the 6X rack, trying to decide which ones I should try on.

I remember the click-click-click of the hangers as she pushed through the clothes. I learned not to say if I liked something; it meant I would never get it. She would throw a few garments at me, order me to try them on, and remind me these were the biggest clothes they made for girls my age and I had better not be getting any fatter.

I'd overheard girls on the playground talking about how they loved to shop with their mommies, getting new clothes and going to the local café after for a treat. It was a very grown-up time, full of secret woman things mothers shared with their daughters. That was not my life. I tried to convince myself it didn't matter.

I learned something important. The fatter I was, the less Father and his friends wanted to do things with *The Girls*. They didn't like my fat either. The fatter I was, the safer I was. Fat was my protection.

To keep my new friend fat happy, I ate. I had a two-hour window between when the school bus dropped me home and Mother arrived from work. Standing in front of the cupboard, I would wonder what to eat to keep fat happy.

I learned how to eat cookies and lollies in packets, taking just enough to indulge, but not enough for Mother to ask where it had gone. Sometimes there weren't sweets, so I had tinned tuna. How boring! I learned that mixing through mayonnaise helped with the flavour. My favourite was taking some powdered sugar and mixing it with butter. Yummy, creamy and fatty. I was learning the fine art of deception.

Mother started taking me to the local Weight Watchers club. She insisted it was because she wanted me to be healthy. But I knew it was because she was sick of having an ugly, fat child. I hated going because I was the only kid there. I knew Mother was determined to get me thin. We would walk in and stand in line to get weighed.

Each week I would get on the scales, and they would hardly budge. The woman doing the weighing would smile, or move the weighted balance, trying to eke out a loss if she could. Even I wasn't sure why I wasn't losing weight. Mother hid all the goodies and treats; I was stuck eating slimy vegetables and a piece of chicken or fish. I still couldn't lose weight.

Mother shook her head, leaned over and whispered to me, 'What have you been getting in to?'

There was one time when Mother came to my rescue, trying to save me from the embarrassment of not losing weight again. I did wonder if it was more about her being embarrassed by me, trying to find an excuse for my failure.

'I'm wondering if it's possible to look at the goal weight you have for Annie?' Mother said sweetly.

The woman looked at Mother, and then at me. 'What do you mean?'

Mother's smile was polite and pointed. 'Well, she is a growing child. I was wondering if, because she is getting taller, you think maybe something needs to be adjusted for her goal weight? I mean, look at her; she looks almost, well, thin.'

The lady behind the desk seemed a bit confused. But then looked at me. 'How about we get your height again? Let's see what that does.'

I stood tall and straight while she pulled out the measure. I had grown several inches.

The woman behind the desk did her calculations. 'Well, there you go. Well done, Annie, you've actually reached your goal weight! Good job.'

Mother was proud. I'm sure it had more to do with the fact she had figured out why I was never reaching my goal weight. And now, finally, her daughter was thin. She was a successful parent.

I enjoyed this new experience of being thin. I remember one day wrapping my arms around my waist and noticing how different my body felt. Instead of a soft pillow, it was a smooth, taut surface. I had curves! Even my breasts were growing. I liked the way it felt. I was 12 and had heard the word sexy before and wondered if this is what it felt like to be sexy. Mother bought me some nice clothes. Was this what it meant to be special? Mother was happy, so I was happy.

It didn't last. I should've known better. We were at a family friend's house. I never really enjoyed going there. The dad was one of Father's friends who used to do things to *The Girls*. We were outside playing in the pool with others, so I was pretty sure nothing could happen. Father and this man were sitting under a tree, drinking beer and laughing. I looked over at them, and this guy was looking at me. He just stared, with a deadpan face, and gave nothing away. It scared me. He started talking to Father, and then they both looked at me. I felt uncomfortable, like I needed to cover myself. I turned away, pretended to laugh at a kid and then ran and did a cannonball into the pool.

That night, Father was sitting in his usual chair. I walked past him on my way to bed. He looked at me and sneered. It was a look I hadn't seen in a long time.

It didn't take long for Father's friends to come back around. They liked my boobs and my curves. I went away. This wasn't my job, and I didn't like these men; they made me feel yuck. So *Runaway Girl* came and had to deal with them.

Things got really hard because I had to choose. I could stay thin and make Mother happy, but then Father and his friends would be at me, which would be horrible. Or I could get fat and keep my body safe, but then Mother wouldn't love me anymore because I wasn't thin. I don't think she cared about what Father's friends did to *The Girls*; she just wanted me to be pretty.

I was a kid, and didn't know a lot, but I knew mothers should protect their daughters. Mine didn't. I was furious but couldn't show it. *Angry Girl* had to own those feelings, but I sure felt it too. I was really confused. How could Mother not care? How could she not protect me?

Those years were really hard. Because I was older, some things happened, well, like I said, *Runaway Girl* dealt with that. But I will say, sometimes I thought we would die because things got so hard.

Angry Girl knew I was mad because Mother didn't protect us, and we figured out how I could get even with her. It was pretty simple really; get fat again. If we got fat, these men would go away. But the best part was it would piss off Mother. *Angry Girl* whispered she was sure this could work.

Mother loved having her Twelfth Night party. Every year, 12 days after Christmas, she would open up the house and invite friends and neighbours in. She would make things like sausage rolls and mince meat pies months before the party and then freeze them. This was the key to pissing her off. I ate them. Not all of them, and not all at once, but just bit by bit. Microwaves weren't around then, so I'd eat them frozen. I told myself it was because I was hungry and they tasted good. *Angry Girl* reminded me we were getting even with Mother. I smiled.

In the end, I was fat again, and I was safe. I told myself it didn't matter if Mother didn't love me. I had learned no matter what I did, I would never be good enough for her.

Attempted Bonding

Mother asked me to sit with her at the kitchen table. Maybe she thought I was grown-up enough to understand what she wanted to say. I'm not sure.

'I have something I want to share with you.' She reached across the table, her long bony fingers cradling a photo she wanted me to look at. It was old and small, a black-and-white photo with scissored edges.

'This is a special photo,' she said.

I was wary as I reached for it, already old enough to understand this was an adult discussion and a weak, pathetic attempt to build some sort of bridge between us. I couldn't think of any other reason for her sharing this photo with me.

I stared at the picture. It was a younger version of Mother and Father; Mother was holding a baby in her arms. Standing by the back of an old Combi pop-up van, they were thin and vibrant and appeared happy. Father was in a singlet and long pants with a belt. Mother was wearing a dress with a plaid pattern, cinched at the waist, showing off her sculpted body. Mother tenderly held the baby, securely wrapped in a light blanket. The baby had jet-black hair. But not ordinary hair; this baby had a scruffy black mohawk, a tuft of hair straight down the middle of their head.

'This is you,' Mother said.

'Really?' I couldn't hide my surprise. I now had pale, mousy brown hair, not black.

'Yes. We were so happy to have you with us.' Her eyes beamed with love as she stared at the image in the photo.

She went on to tell me how I got my name. She and Father had decided when I was born that if I had dark hair, I would be called by my middle name, Annie. If I had light hair, they would use my first name, Margaret. I came into this world with a jet-black mohawk, so Annie it was.

Mother brimmed with pride as she told me about how my birth was a blessing and a treasure. She loved my two older brothers but was desperate for a daughter. Mother had miscarried twice, and both were girls. In her retelling, I was the long-awaited gift. Her eyes shone with pride and affection as she stared at the picture and told me her story.

This idealised beginning was a mental conundrum for me. I still remembered how she treated me as a child; her loathing of my very existence, and the beatings she gave me, physical and emotional, because I did not meet her exacting standards. And yet somehow, now, she saw me as a blessing? I was confused.

Did I want to believe mothers innately love their children, no matter what? Or, more practically, was she telling me this when I had lost a significant amount of weight, and suddenly I was the daughter she wanted? Was she finally proud of me? When I was thin, tall and elegant, she could parade me before her friends and say, see...this is *my* daughter. Somehow wiping from her mind the way my world would implode in order to meet her need for a thin, beautiful daughter.

Reflecting on my origin stories as an adult became important pieces in the puzzle of my life. Like this rendition of how she and Father had chosen to use my middle name as if it was something intimately tying us to each other, as though the choice itself proved her love. Did she not see the years of abuse and how it affected me? In her mind, was it practical, even logical? All she could see was her need. By sharing this intimate detail, she was somehow showing me proof of her love—a mother's need to love and be loved. It was an imperfect love at best, but surely, despite everything that happened, she loved me. Was this the magic of motherhood—looking beyond all the problems and clinging to an image of the love she wanted from me? And in her case, would my love for her somehow be a forgiveness of our history?

Somewhere in the far recesses of my brain, I was beginning to understand a small corner of my existence. It was something I was desperate for, to make sense of the chaos of my life. All the physical abuse and verbal degradation were her attempt to love me, even when she was fundamentally incapable.

How It Began

It would be years later, when seeing a therapist, that I would understand how much of my rebellious behaviour and lack of direction during my young adult years resulted from living with Multiple Personality Disorder (MPD). I was *Annie* to everyone around me. It was on the boat trip to America when I became—hiding away Maggie, the core, the original child who was born. I was protecting her from a life of trauma. Even when the abuse had ceased and we were safe, I stayed. I wanted my own existence.

My desire for a life unlike my childhood was thwarted; I remained tethered to my trauma and responsible for managing the system—*The Girls*. I had overseen our survival, including a mother who despised me and a rotation of abuse the system had to live with. What I couldn't see was how *The Girls* continued to affect my life, even after I left home. Because I was naturally dissociative, I forgot most of our childhood, including *The Girls*. But the residual effects of anger, angst and anxiety continued to haunt me.

A few clouds in the sky and a slight breeze coming off the foothills of the Rockies sent a chill through my bones, reminding me there could still be late snow before summer. This was the majestic location of the Bible college where I was enjoying my second year. When friends from my church in Texas told me about this school, I jumped at the opportunity. Admittedly, it was as much about escaping the growing tension of being around my family as it was about learning biblical principles and applying those in a higher education setting. From the late nights in the student union, to meals in the cafeteria and study habits (or lack thereof), it was all about my choices—my wants and dreams—which did not include my family.

When the bell rang for the end of class, like an army of ants, everyone moved to the school chapel for our weekly assembly. Usually, a school professor or an area pastor would speak to us about our commitment to studies, reminding us to use this education and our gifts to serve God. It was something I heartily agreed with but always found hard to listen to. Men stood in the pulpit and preached these messages, ultimately ensuring the graduates they churned out met their particular brand of Christian service. We were required to dress smartly, obey study hours and do our homework and chores.

I found these restrictions tedious and cumbersome. It felt like I had gone from one set of rules at home to another. I had been so ready to put my family behind me; I gave no thought to how these new rules might affect me, regularly getting into trouble for breaking school rules (going out after curfew and not showing up for dorm meetings were my favourite acts of rebellion). I would be called into the Dean's office and suffer gentle but coerced consequences.

Somehow, I made one real friend, Kate. She tolerated my behaviour and looked past my foibles and rash choices. A few years later, after seeing a therapist (shrink #2 at this point) I told her about my MPD diagnosis. It made no difference. She said she always found me to be an interesting friend. Her acceptance of me, of *us*, was the first time I ever felt truly understood.

On this sunny spring day, I entered the chapel with the rest of the students; I looked around to see if Kate was already there. We often sat together towards the back. I saw her blonde curls a few rows up and plonked into the seat next to her. Minimal greetings—just a simple, comfortable acknowledgement of each other's presence.

The school president opened in prayer and then told us we had a special guest today from a mission organisation. I think his name was Jason. He shared the opportunity to spend a summer in the Philippines, working with the locals. Having always wanted to live overseas (another desire to escape my family, perhaps?), I was engrossed as I listened to him talk about making a difference in a developing country.

I knew nothing about the Philippines other than it was an exotic Asian country on the other side of the world. Jason told us about this place called The Dump in the capital city of Manila, where people lived—literally—on a dump, scavenging for food and things they could sell to eke out an existence. We heard about children living on the streets, homeless and, too often, lured into the sex trade. He showed us a video with images challenging white privilege attitudes, making me realise how much I took for granted.

At the end, Jason encouraged us to be part of this work. I looked at Kate; she had been as struck as I was by the presentation. We both grabbed information and promised to catch up at the end of classes to talk.

I was so excited! All I could think about the rest of the day was the Philippines. The Asia Pacific! Wow! I was a country girl from Texas (with vague British roots). The Philippines was a world away from my Central Texas upbringing. The opportunity to live and work in a different culture seemed like an adventure! I was excited to consider how this equatorial voyage would change me.

Kate and I caught up later in the day to talk about it. Both giddy with excitement at the possibility, we talked nonstop about what this opportunity could mean for us. Something ran deep for me. I couldn't define it, but I knew this trip would be a significant signpost in my life. There was joy in having this adventure with Kate—it would be wonderful to share it with someone I was close to. Underneath it all, something began ticking in my heart. A quiet thing, a gentle murmur I could not yet identify.

This was how my journey towards motherhood began—finding purpose in something outside myself, rather than resenting the murky cloud of my childhood. Here, it was about helping the people of the Philippines. I raised money to cover my costs, asking friends and churches to sponsor me. The Bible college also pitched in to help cover expenses. In the end, I quickly raised the funds needed to make this momentous trip a reality.

My attitude towards the school changed. I began developing a sense of self. Kate and I would get together regularly to discuss our plans and pray over the next steps, from raising funds, to the families we would stay with in the Philippines and for our teammates. Every step of this journey felt like it was what I was supposed to do. From financial support to paperwork and orientation, it all fell into place seamlessly. I was learning to be independent, deciding things about my life without the input of the Parents.

I was growing up.

Kate and I gave each other an excited goodbye hug at the end of term. We would each have a brief time at home before meeting up in Southern California, where we would have our final orientation and training, along with 50 or so other students, preparing for our time in the Philippines.

The Filipino Way

Before I knew it, I was flying into LAX, on my way to orientation at Biola University in Southern California. Over 50 of us had travelled from across the US and Canada to be part of this experience.

During orientation week, someone told us in one of our many meetings that we would feel like someone had wrapped a warm wet blanket around us upon arrival in Manila. No words could have been truer. The moment we disembarked, I could feel the humidity penetrating my clothes, becoming a sticky residue on my skin. But how I loved it!

They divided us into smaller teams to spread out across the northern island of Luzon. Kate and I deliberately worked on different teams. It would give us the opportunity to come together during our breaks to share our experiences. It was during these times, when we would room together, swapping stories of what we had learned and how the people of the Philippines had affected us.

I was lucky to be teamed up with two Canadians, Todd and Phil. Apparently, during our week of orientation in Southern California, the leadership was confident I could cope as the only female on the team. Todd and Phil were a hoot, and we worked well together. After our week of acclimatising in Manila (where hotel rooms spewed brown tap water and cockroaches were our intimate neighbours), we were sent by bus to our postings. Todd, Phil and I went to Dagupan City, a beachside regional area, to be hosted by local families, immersing ourselves in the culture.

When I arrived at my accommodation, I stayed with a lovely family who were well-off by Filipino standards. They wanted to feed me fried chicken and other American food to make me feel at home. I became the artful dodger and begged them to feed me Filipino-style. In exchange, I promised I would teach them a few Tex-Mex recipes (a spicy mix of the flavours of Texas and Mexico). We spent many happy hours in their kitchen, where I learned to make *adobo* and *pancit*, and how to cook rice properly, teaching them English phrases during these cooking sessions, which inevitably led to much laughter and giggling. I quickly lost the need for cutlery and learned that my hand, with rice, was about the best eating utensil around. I was embracing the culture and loving it.

It was easy to relax in this laid-back Filipino way, where even my OCD tendencies regarding time seemed to go on holiday. It didn't matter if you were half an hour, or even an hour late. Time was a fluid concept in Filipino culture. For church services, meetings—anything—being on time simply did not factor into their day. This meant I learned to stop and relax, spending time on my front porch, reading and watching large geckos keeping mosquitoes at bay, smiling at the occasional chicken rummaging for bugs in the nearby bushes. There was no need to rush. I was comfortable in this culture in a way I had never felt growing up in Texas. My anxiety, an integral part of my daily life, seemed to melt away.

I made sense of cold bucket showers, coming to treasure the relief they provided. Where I lived, we were fortunate to have a tap in the shower, which filled a garbage bin with water. The idea was to use a large scoop and drench yourself, soap up, rinse and repeat. The logic was simple and invigorating. It was hot; it was humid. Who wouldn't want a refreshing cool shower?

It wasn't a flawless country. I struggled with *balut*, a cooked duck egg eaten between 14- and 17-days gestation (full gestation being 21 days). I once watched someone eat one; they slurped up the gelatinous liquid, the delicate tiny feathers of the dead duckling visible. Nor did the caged dogs go down well with me. Dogs in cages along the roadside would end up on someone's dinner table. I knew this country wasn't perfect. But I refused to let these cultural differences impede my relationship with the Filipino people.

Everything about this country entranced me: lush tropical mountains and white sandy beaches. Even the stench of city streets, with poverty and desolation everywhere, called to me. I became enamoured by the simple lifestyle and contentedness of these people. It was a stark contrast to the complicated world I came from.

In the end, it was the people who captured my heart. The smiling faces, playfulness and eager interactions held a joy I had not seen in my Western culture. They valued relationships, where the West seemed to value *stuff*. All of this beguiled and entranced me. I was drawn to their simple lives with wood and dirt floors, milk crates for furniture and foam mattresses for beds where up to three or four would sleep. Children were everywhere, from the streets and slums of Manila to the dirt tracks of the mountains. Many had parents. Some lived with aunties and uncles (*Tita* and *Tito*), and even more just roamed the streets, begging for food and sleeping in crates and dark nooks and crannies. Children played on the streets with tin cans and old rocks, a stark contrast to what I knew. They would run up, curious to see a stranger with white skin, and then skip off with a giggle when I said hello.

I couldn't help but contrast my upbringing, full of emotional poverty, with the lives I encountered every day on the streets of the Philippines. Was I jealous? Despite the conditions many lived in, they were content, even joyful. I found this ability to accept their circumstances and still find hope refreshing.

Then, I saw her face. She couldn't have been more than three. Short wispy hair, big brown eyes, holding a stick as she kicked rocks down the road. She stopped and stared at me, standing up straight. Her old dress was dirty and ripped, but still she stood proud—almost defiant. Her big brown eyes stared straight into my soul as a smile gradually crept across her face. She waved at me, giggling and laughing as she ran down the road.

That was the moment. It was when I knew the Filipino people would always be a part of my life. I would adopt a child from the Philippines. I didn't know the path; I had no clue as to the process or how it would happen. But I felt a surety in my soul about my future.

Re-Entry

It is not uncommon to experience culture shock when travelling to a new country. You leave behind, even for a short time, the familiar and safe things of home. Stepping into a new world, change is required; habits and thought processes have to fit into another culture. Differences might include respect for elders, the treatment of women, transportation, and even the food. Just about anything could be a challenge, depending on the country. And when thrown together, this can cause culture shock.

Instead, I experienced reverse culture shock. I became so immersed in the Filipino way that when I came back, all those things I should have found comforting — the familiar routines—none of it was grounding. I wasn't at home in my own culture. It wasn't noticeable at first. I spent my early weeks recounting experiences and sharing stories with others—a vicarious way of staying anchored in memories of the Philippines. This gradual re-entry hid from me the full magnitude of the tidal wave looming on my horizon.

In true dissociative style, my system had hidden itself from me for much of my young adult life. But somehow, the emotional toll of returning from the gentle pace of the Philippines, being blindsided by an inability to settle back into a Western culture, triggered my system.

I would later realise it was one of my alters, *Angry Woman*, a very social justice oriented alter that loved our time in the Philippines, who struggled the most. A return to a white-privileged lifestyle frustrated her. This meant I lost control, and things began to fall apart. It wasn't cognitive; I didn't know it was *Angry Woman*, but something shifted. My dissatisfaction with the status quo made everything around me feel wrong and incomplete, frustrating me. The poverty and subsistence I encountered confronted and challenged me—changed me. I found the resilience and simple joys embodied in the Filipino people a salve for my Western heart.

I was back at college, going to class and walking across the quad, a wide concrete path cutting a line through the broad sea of grass that reminded me of the streets of Dagupan City. In my mind, I returned to those streets, where tricycles barrelled down asphalt roads and schoolgirls walked arm in arm, giggling, umbrellas keeping the fierce equatorial sun off their young skin. Then I would imagine the faces of small children staring at me. These images would come back to me repeatedly, in waves, creating a sensory overload of smells and sounds, causing a cacophony in my brain.

The resentment set in. I would go to dinner in the school cafeteria and our plates would be piled high with more mixed vegetable and Salisbury steak than three people could afford to eat on any given day in the Philippines. I would watch students (including myself) get up from the table and take half-finished plates of food to the bin. The waste when others were starving or, at best, living off a meagre handful of cooked rice each day made me—made *Angry Woman*—seethe.

My clothing changed. The school dress code for girls was a dress or smart pants and a nice shirt. Someone always had an ironing board set up somewhere in the dorm to remove last-minute wrinkles from shirts. I had embraced casual dress in the Philippines and kept it up when I returned. There was no smartness in my dress; it was about comfort. Pushing every boundary with these rules, I wore loose-fitting pants and shirts, and I certainly didn't care about wrinkles. I passed the dress code—just—so got away with it.

I was desperate to hang on to the memories of my time in the Philippines, where the people, land, and way of life had stolen my heart. It was a strum in my soul that would mellow over the years, but never entirely go away. I would follow the news with keen interest for anything happening in the Philippines, whether political or meteorological. I watched in despair as the eruption of Mt. Pinatubo destroyed village after village. Typhoons were the worst. So many people lived in shanties, unable to withstand the ferocious rain and winds. Homes, and lives, lost.

It always came back to the people. It was the face of that little girl, a street urchin, who captured my soul, making me hope for a day when I could adopt a child from the Philippines. A child to love and nurture in a way I had never known.

My dream of living in the Philippines and adopting felt like it was slipping through my fingers. Done with school, I climbed onto the proverbial wheel of life. I refocused, setting aside my dream, losing myself in work, bills and a social life. My fondness for the Philippines remained, but only if I allowed myself to look at it.

Puzzle Pieces

I wandered, uncomfortable in my own skin. I rattled between friendships, faith and an inability to settle. My sense of self eroded as I questioned my reason for being, trying to find my place in this thing called life. This was my biggest challenge—trying to figure out who I was. I watched friends peel off into serious relationships and careers where they knew exactly what they wanted. It came easily for them, but not for me. I worked at mindless jobs, always hoping the next one would be fulfilling. Slapping on a happy face, I socialised, pretending my lack of direction didn't matter. I was free and single. I should have been living my best life. Deep down, I was beginning to wonder what was wrong with me.

When I was at my lowest, I made futile attempts to return to the Philippines, thinking it would solve my problems. Doors slammed shut for reasons I did not want to acknowledge. I applied to a mission organisation only to find out all my references said I was not suitable for the rigours of overseas life. My referee's lack of transparency was devastating. But in my heart, I knew they were right. Bouncing between overwhelming rage and isolation, I felt completely out of control.

A type of paranoia seemed to set in. It felt as though I was watching myself react to situations, unable to control my responses. I bounced between low-level clerk roles, trying to claw back some sense of value and worth, which only made me more volatile. I became a social recluse, refusing invitations to go out to dinner or movies, fearful of how I might respond if something triggered me. Contentment eluded me.

I was grieving, watching my dream of living in the Philippines slip through my fingers. I berated myself for thinking I had the right to live there, or that adopting a Filipino child was something I deserved.

Twice in my young adult life, people I respected urged me to see a therapist. They saw the anger and authority issues I had. I couldn't see the need for objective help, but they did.

Hindsight would show me that if those doors hadn't slammed shut on returning to the Philippines, if I had instead sidestepped my erratic behaviour, I would never have been forced to face the truth of my life. My ignorance had me believing it was simply a matter of self-discipline. I needed to control my anger and anxiety issues. The truth of my life was unfolding.

I saw my first therapist while I lived in Colorado. He was kind and compassionate, but I was not willing or able to come to terms with what was happening in my soul. I avoided my family, the distance between us giving me a convenient excuse not to see them. The very idea of spending time with them riddled me with anxiety, leading to confusion and volatile behaviour. I didn't understand what was going on, or the connection between family and emotions. I couldn't bring myself to discuss this in therapy.

After my disappointing attempt to return to the Philippines, I eventually moved back to Texas, a mere four hours from the family. I felt the pressure to return home and spend time with them. Every time they called, asking when I was coming home for a visit, I felt the noose tighten ever so slightly. I spent years trying to extricate myself from their clutches. Especially Mother. Her neediness and desire to rekindle a relationship with me created a visceral reaction in my body. I was grateful there was a physical distance between us. Often after talking with Mother on the phone, I would put the handset down and desperately try to shake off the chains I felt tieing me to her. I got on with my dull, drab, disappointing life, railing against God and anyone who would listen about how unfair life was. I didn't think I was asking for much. I was desperate to return to the Philippines and loose myself in the people and culture.

My emotional issues came to the forefront again, so I quickly started seeing another therapist. As I began to trust myself and my therapist, I realised my childhood had been anything but normal. My angst about being with family had moved beyond visceral sensations to actual memories. These would become important pieces of the puzzle of my life, helping me re-create, as best I could, my checkered and vague history. It gave me a small glimmer of sanity in those moments when I felt like I was barely surviving.

Often, those memories were ugly and full of fear. In the safety of my therapist's office, they would come charging at me like stampeding elephants. I began to remember a childhood full of abuse from both Mother and Father. Slowly, too slowly at times, pieces of the erratic puzzle of my life began falling into place. I began understanding that my angry, anxiety-ridden behaviour, was a type of self-preservation, a protection of sorts, which was all-consuming. It also explained much of my binge-eating behaviour, my need to control something in my life, even if it was an illusion at best. I struggled to believe this foggy history could be behind my behaviour. I came to understand this was a phase many trauma survivors go through, trying to explain away the truth of their memories, because they don't want to believe this could happen to them.

Just as important was discovering I lived with MPD. It was something new to me—strange, weird. I was terrified people would think I was psychotic. Apparently, there was a tribe of people who lived inside me and were part of helping us survive as a child. As *Annie*, I was not fully aware of my role in the system; I thought I had always existed. I just lived my life, leaning on this therapist who helped me come to terms with this diagnosis and creative form of survival. Years later, I understood Maggie had created me as a child alter to shield our body from the abuse it endured. I was going through the motions, trying to come to terms with the complexities of my life.

In my dissociation, I hid the abuse away, remembering only a history of a mother who was disengaged; she was a woman who preferred painting in her art corner or drinking with friends. I was a fat, disappointing child, pushed aside and ignored. The only things I knew about mothering were from my fraught relationship with a woman who I believed did not want me. This information, these memories of my childhood, were a conundrum, creating waves of cognitive dissonance.

And while I was grateful for friends who encouraged me to seek help, it was a hard-fought brutal battle to come to terms with the lived reality of my life.

There were other friends who carved out a place for my inconsistent and chaotic behaviour. When looking back on those days, I understand the dissociative state that I existed in. Times when I would call them in the middle of the night, in absolute fear of what was happening in my brain. They would quickly wrap me in the security of their friendship, sitting with me, asking occasional questions and allowing me to process the jumbled mess in my head. It was as if the stabilising ingredient was someone I could trust. I will forever be thankful for the place of safety and peace they provided for me.

I began to understand the truth of what my childhood had been. I intrinsically owned Mother's loathing of my very existence, replaying her tapes about how I was fat and ugly, and how she wished I'd never been born. The physical and emotional betrayal ran deep in my soul like a muddy river, knowing I would never meet her exacting standards.

And yet somehow there were memories of love and care. Vague images of Christmas presents and fairy lights. Hair washing, where just feeling the touch of her skin on mine melted my heart and soothed my soul.

Could she have had her own unresolved childhood full of abuse and neglect, which blinded and controlled her? Was Father abusive to her? Did he coercively control her? Could she only see her needs, a matter of some warped sense of survival? As a young mother, she wished for a perfect daughter; later she wrestled with her own frailties, trying to claw back the lost years with me. Did she do this out of a need to love and be loved? I dared to wonder: was the abuse she subjected me to her own futile attempt to love me? An imperfect love at best, but could it mean that despite what happened, she loved me?

I don't believe I ever consciously asked these questions, at least not at first. The need and craving for her love flowed through my bones, justified because of genetics. It had a firm grip on me. The pain, the emptiness of needing her love so strong at times, I thought it would strangle me.

I wanted to understand our relationship, even though I feared it. Somewhere in the far recesses of my brain, convoluted memories kept boiling over, unconsciously making sense of a small corner of my life.

Through all the therapy and self-discovery, I became content in my singleness. It's what I told myself, repeatedly. From accepting my lack of desirability to wanting my independence from the shackles of my past, the veneer of acceptance made my history palatable.

I never considered that marriage, let alone raising a family, could be part of my life. It was easier to find contentment on my own rather than considering the complexities of marriage and motherhood. Honestly, with the example of my life, was it any wonder I found the idea of being a mother a non-starter?

But. I had been to the Philippines and fallen in love with the people and their happy-go-lucky ways. Although I only vaguely sensed it at the time, a motherhood seed was planted in my heart, and I longed to parent one of these beautiful Filipino children. And not out of some white coloniser perspective built around rescuing them to provide a better life, but to love a child who deserved love and to be loved in return. This quiet flame of motherhood ignited in my soul.

How was I supposed to reconcile the truth of this growing desire in my heart to one day be a parent with my own abusive history? It was something I could not easily answer, and, as with many things in my life I could not wrestle with, I simply let it sit, hoping by getting on with my life, it would naturally work itself out.

Single-Minded

With years of therapy, my heart softened. I was relieved. Satisfied. With the help of a therapist, things changed. What I couldn't predict, what I didn't understand yet, was the impact my relationship with Mother would have on me. The quiet and insidious way she gave me up to be used by Father and his friends sat like a lead weight on my heart.

I questioned everything about her. There was no rhyme or reason in my brain, just simply—why? Why didn't she love me? What did I do to deserve this treatment? Irrational perspectives dogged me as I blamed myself for what had happened. I was desperate to unravel these questions, believing it would make sense of my life.

I was gradually becoming content in my single life (it's what I told myself). Therapy was a constant. Sometimes overwhelming, but I managed, knowing this balance of working through my personal crap and having a real life was a healthy place to be.

Between a job I was enjoying and an apartment of my own, I was independent, relishing my freedom. The food in my refrigerator, my clothes, my car—they were all bought with my money. These were my choices—the good and the bad. All mine.

I was moving beyond some of my trust issues, trying to come out of my introverted ways and make a few friends. Admittedly, it was still easier to be alone in my apartment, listening to music or watching something on my second-hand TV. I would relax on the couch with my cats. They were my best friends and, apart from mealtime, they never asked for anything and were happy to cuddle up with me. Being an introvert suited me well.

What I relished most were holidays with my dear friend Kate. We would travel and visit new and interesting locations. We didn't have to go far. For us, it was about being together and the connection we shared. We spent time in the Canadian Rockies, hiking and taking pictures of wildlife and glaciers. Another time we went to Sanibel Island, just off the west coast of Florida, hunting shells by day and enjoying rich conversation each evening (usually over cards or dice and a bottle of wine). There was always somewhere new to explore, and even though we lived apart, every time we were together, it was as if no time had passed. The conversation always flowed. Kate was a stable presence for me, where I could talk about anything and feel safe. The freedom of my single life was great.

Period Pain

I was in my late 20s when I began having problems with my period. Cramps made me double over in pain, with headaches requiring medication and hours under the covers just to survive. I was bleeding heavily; tampons and pads barely kept ahead of the blood loss. I was constantly tired and worn out and went to see a gynaecologist. I was ignorant of the practical brutality which lay ahead.

I was almost 30 and had never had a Pap smear, which made sense. Mother never took me under her nurturing wing, providing me with a woman's perspective of how my body was changing. I vaguely remember when I started my period we discussed how, since I was bleeding, my life would change. She may have even been teary. But this was not followed by any practical expertise to help me with the new hormonal imbalances in my life. She gave me no real-world insight into using sanitary pads or tampons. It was all up to me.

So, when I lay on the examination table, body covered, legs spread wide in stirrups, I was terrified. The odd draught made my naked skin shiver. I was embarrassed, nervous, humiliated. Who wouldn't be? Just seeing the long, thin speculum convinced me the doctor was using some sort of medieval torture device. The cold, hard object invaded my body, and my muscles constricted instinctively as he widened the device and locked it in place.

'I need you to relax for me. This will hurt more if you don't.' I am sure his scale of pain was far broader than mine. My body jerked as he tried to take the sample. The sharp pain, unexpected.

'I need you to hold still, please.' He went in again. This time, I knew the pain would come and held myself rigid.

'Done. Go ahead and sit up.'

He rolled his stool away, slipping my legs out of the stirrups. I pulled the not quite big enough sheet across my legs, dangling them over the edge of the table.

'You okay?' He asked, moving over to the sink to wash his hands.

'Yeah. I just didn't realise it would hurt so much.'

He took his notepad and sat on the stool in front of me, writing a few notes. He looked up. 'My apologies. I'm not used to dealing with, well, clients who are so, umm, large. It made it harder for me to get the sample.'

And there was the truth—it was my fault. Something went wrong, and I was to blame.

My thinking went something like this. I was fat because I ate. I ate to comfort myself when memories of my childhood overwhelmed me. Therefore, being fat was my fault, the abuse was my fault, and the pain from the examination was my fault. This was something I was good at—accepting fault and exonerating everyone else.

The doctor had already moved on, unaware of what his words had done to me. 'Were you abused in your childhood?'

'Yep.' I hid my surprise at his directness—although in retrospect I shouldn't have been. I refused to share more than I had to, no matter how much I should have trusted his skill and knowledge. He was a medical professional I was paying to help me, no more.

He sighed. 'There are scars indicating you experienced prolonged sexual abuse.' He was stating a fact, but really it was a question.

'Yes, that's correct.'

'Okay. Why don't you get dressed and come down to my office when you're ready.'

He disappeared.

I self-consciously pulled on my jeans and shirt. He was a doctor. Cognitively, I knew he saw women in various stages of nakedness on a daily basis. But he saw my body and said I was fat, making it worse. His words were a judgement. I walked into his office, where he was making notes. He looked up and pointed to the chair across from his desk. I had barely sat down when he informed me the scarring in my vagina would have lifelong ramifications.

Sex would be a painful experience. He pulled out his trusty model of a vagina, beginning a lengthy discourse about the scar tissue on my vaginal wall and how it would not be pliable during intercourse. Second, it would make getting pregnant hard. Not impossible, but highly unlikely. Again, the scarring would make it difficult for the sperm to complete their trip to my Fallopian tubes.

I found his bedside manner direct and clinical. He was there to provide his perspective, not ask me how I felt about this revelation. His job was to impart information, not see to my emotional welfare.

This was how I justified his behaviour. It was simply another consequence of my childhood. I couldn't do anything about it, so there was no reason to be upset.

I left his office with a script for the pill to regulate my inconsistent periods and make my blood flow lighter. It worked on both accounts. The other information about internal scarring and the emotional ramifications of this news would be left for the therapist's couch.

Talking to my therapist about this news forced me to face more of the ugly truth of my life. Vacillating towards denial was easy for me. I was desperate to believe I had made it all up and pretended the abuse never happened. The medical nature of my problems was a line in the sand, an affirmation of the veracity of the images and memories I had started working through. Those scars spoke loudly of the reality of a childhood I could not deny.

Somewhere in my head, I sensed a flood of relief. I was confounded. I knew the stories; it was at this point I was supposed to feel grief about not being able to birth a child of my own, feel an agonising emptiness because of the loss of this motherly function, forever ripped from me. Instead, a sense of relief washed over me, and I felt grateful the physical act of childbirth would not be something I would have to wrestle with.

Closure. It was a hard-fought full stop on my history. It put so much into perspective. I could not deny the abuse and had to work through it, grateful for a therapist to walk this journey with me. I started coming to terms with some of my coping mechanisms (although I found them humiliating to admit). I wasn't grieving. Instead, I was rebuilding, understanding the truth of who I was. And just as important, I would build any family I had through adoption. I quietly allowed my heart to contemplate whether the dream I had in the Philippines almost a decade before might become a reality.

All this discovery about my history and coming to terms with my life were my first baby steps towards motherhood. I was starting to remove the shackles and chains of my past, opening my arms to the possibility of loving and nurturing a child.

A Whole New World

I was not looking for a romantic relationship. I lived for the weekends, with friends and church. Women over 30 seemed to think they had passed their prime if they weren't married—this was not my perspective. I had given up on the dream and just wanted to be happy in my own skin (thank you, therapy!). It didn't mean I wasn't lonely. I was sometimes, and jealous too. I watched friends get married, happy for them, but I did not aspire for a relationship to make me complete.

And then, on 23 December 1995, I met Tom.

We met online, back in the dark ages, when Internet connectivity in homes was rare and mobile phones were the size of a brick. I instinctively avoided technology.

Part of my job required me to send files and data to our head office via the Internet. I became a quick learner, discovering chat rooms where I would linger after work with my takeaway dinner, settling in for an evening of lurking around chat rooms, investigating this thing called the World Wide Web.

One late December evening, I logged into the Christian Interactive Network (CIN), and there was Tom. His profile showed interests in religion and sci-fi. We talked for hours about his home, Australia.

Before I knew it, Tom and I had exchanged emails. Long, expensive phone calls quickly followed. His work took him to Canada, allowing us to plan time together. I picked him up at the Dallas Ft Worth Airport the first time we met. We behaved like giddy, tentative teenagers, our nerves taking over. During our few days together, we became more comfortable with each other, daring brief touches, confirming the reality of us. Our relationship escalated quickly. I travelled to Canada, and he came to Texas frequently. Friends interrogated him extensively; sure he was using me to get US residency. Others worried he might be an axe-wielding murderer. It was a whirlwind romance, full of new and exciting feelings.

I, Maggie, disappeared at the age of three on our family's transatlantic trip to the States. It was *Annie* who lived and breathed, moving this body through its daily routine. *Annie* who managed a childhood saturated with trauma, deciding who came out when, to handle different abuse. She even took the abuse on herself, if she felt this served the best purposes of the system.

After leaving home and mapping out some semblance of a shadowed and protected young adult life, I, Maggie, remained cocooned away in the safety of dissociation. I was asleep and unaware of the romantic attachment *Annie* had formed with Tom and the stress this was causing *The Girls*.

For *Annie*, it had been a long slow burn. She knew the physical intimacy of the relationship with Tom terrified *The Girls*. For her, the excitement his touch elicited, these overwhelming sensations and feelings exploding in *Annie*'s veins, were an unfamiliar experience. In all this, she began to realise she was betraying *The Girls*. By embracing these romantic notions, *The Girls* felt they were being abused again. A man's touch was terrifying. *Annie* refused to discuss it with the system. Instead, she ignored their pleas and enjoyed these new feelings—the gentle touch and excitement—telling herself this must be love.

Somewhere between the romantic allure of this relationship with Tom and the realities of a traumatic family history, I returned.

It was during an afternoon on a beach outside of Galveston, Texas. *Annie* and Tom had taken a long romantic walk, laughing and holding hands as they talked about a future together and what it might look like. Would they live in Texas, where *Annie* had a job? Move to the West Coast—Tom's preference—hoping the IT industry would provide him unlimited opportunities? Or would she return with him to Australia?

Succumbing to their feelings, and doing what *Annie* thought felt natural, they gave way to the excitement and tension of this physical connection. For *Annie,* this would be her first consensual sexual experience. She was nervous as she and Tom embraced in the back seat of her car. In the background, *Annie* could hear the cries of *The Girls*, as they felt like they were being forced to relive their abuse, unsafe from this man *Annie* had formed an attachment to. No matter how hard she tried to put the feelings of the moment first, she could not get away from *The Girls*. Rushes of embarrassment and shame washed over her. She was wreaking havoc on the lives entrusted to her protection, breaking her promise to always keep *The Girls* safe. It was her ultimate selfish act of betrayal.

Doing what was second nature for her, she dissociated, which in this circumstance meant she left, forcing me to return and manage the body. I felt *Annie* as she passed me, her shoulder barely touching mine. She didn't look at me, leaving to hide away with her engulfing sense of failure. She went further inward than I had ever been, desperate for the respite these dark and quiet places could offer.

I felt like I was relaxing in the gentle current under a deep sea, my body slowly rising to the surface with each exhale. Reality came into focus. It was calm at first, a quiet awareness I was no longer asleep. My world was changing. The closer I came to the surface, the closer I was to *Annie* and the more aware I was of Tom.

I drank in as much detail as I could in this gradual return to consciousness, grateful for a slow shift, for the ability to comprehend and make sense of *Annie's* existence thus far. The physical touching ceased, both Tom and I sensing something was amiss. There was no real discussion. Instead, straightening shirts, tucking in pants and steady breathing. I noted he cradled my hand in his. This intimate gesture was a strange sensation; holding hands with someone I did not know, but who thought they knew me.

There was something natural, logical even, in my return. I was the original child. This body, with whatever it had been through, was, in the end, mine. I was the child born; I was the child who went to sleep. With my return, this would once again be my life.

The beauty of dissociation meant I didn't skip a beat. Enough of *Annie's* memories and experiences lingered for me to piecemeal together a basic existence, allowing me to find my way in this new world order. I had gone to sleep at the age of three and was now back, 30 years later. My goal became to mimic *Annie*; be the person Tom knew and was falling in love with. It was as if I was slipping into a coat that was full of *Annie*'s memories, experiences and talents. I was buoyed in the strength of attachment I felt to her.

By wearing her existence, I could walk through her job responsibilities with ease. Tom didn't know, it would be years before I told him of this shift. Friends, associates, even Kate; no one knew. I was imbued with my natural ability to dissociate. I'm not sure I even consciously wrestled with this, apart from a sense of embarrassment, which I quickly set aside (dissociation!). I set my heart and mind on this existence I had resumed, determined to make this life—my relationship with Tom—my own, with *Annie*'s life as a historical reference point.

Tom and I (Maggie) had lengthy discussions about our future, specifically about family and children. We both wanted kids. We had talked about my history (well, *Annie*'s really, but ownership was now my responsibility), and Tom understood how the trauma my body endured meant getting pregnant would be difficult, if not impossible.

Tom didn't baulk at all at the idea of adoption. But, being the ever-pragmatic person he was, we talked about other options like IVF, surrogacy or just simply giving it a good old college try. When I explained the situation completely, painted a picture of what the gynaecologist had told me (*Annie*) about the internal scarring and difficulties associated with getting pregnant, reality hit him. I am sure there was sadness. He wanted a gaggle of miniature versions of himself running around, a testament to his male veracity, a legacy of his own genetic history and heritage. My journey was not so straightforward. Adoption was more than just a consideration of my fertility concerns. I regaled him with stories of my (again, *Annie's*) time in the Philippines and how important adoption was for me in building our family.

After hearing all this, Tom didn't bat an eye. What mattered to him was creating a family together, no matter how it was done.

Within six months, we were married, spending our honeymoon in Australia, where I met his family. The plan was for me to return to Texas while he put in his paperwork to immigrate to the US. What became apparent was it would take years for Tom to get his US residency, while my ability to move to Australia would be unimpeded.

I returned to the States alone and began applying for my visa to immigrate to Australia. I would move Down Under, leaving behind my family and my past, finally free (or so I thought). Tom and I would begin making a future, a home, and a family. Together.

TRUTH WILL OUT

Hiccups

I relished the move to Australia. I was me, Maggie, not the hidden away child who *Annie* had protected.

I made several choices when I moved to Australia, not the least of which was that *Annie*'s diagnosis of MPD would not be a part of my life. Therapy was a nonstarter for me. I believed that this move, literally to the other side of the world, would remove any vestiges of my life with MPD, *Annie*, *The Girls*—all of it—it would simply fade away. I would have a new focus and a new purpose. Therapy had been *Annie*'s guiding light, but it would not be mine. I chose to be free.

I was also determined Tom and I would be the perfect couple, and, when the time came, would raise perfect children. I was a dutiful wife, becoming obsessive, even co-dependent, about making Tom happy. And too, believing once children arrived, our lives would be all about them. This was all rather subliminally driven by a determination not to be the sort of parent Mother was. I would pour everything I had into my children and ensure they felt loved. The preposterous expectations I placed on myself for perfection were setting me up for failure.

If I looked inside, I could sense *Annie*, but I did not see her. It was as if she too understood this was my life now. This was a pragmatic place from which to start my new life, and I emotionally swept her out of my consciousness, sure this would give me a fresh start. I wanted to believe I was free, but instead my dissociation manifested itself in other ways through my insecurities and compulsive need to make Tom happy. Because I did not talk about this fresh start I had chosen, he had no idea, accepting my behaviour as my way of showing my commitment to our marriage.

Tom and I settled in Sydney, eventually opening a web development company. This was in the early days of the Internet boom, when everyone was scrambling to make their squillions from this exciting new industry. Tom was in his element; the tech opportunities delighted him. I felt like I was out of my depth, adjusting to a new marriage and an unfamiliar country. I initially worked for a temporary agency, doing various administration jobs. But I had no direction, no purpose or drive, still trying to figure out what I wanted to do. And now I was also running a small, burgeoning web development company. Truthfully, I was still coming to terms with my existence, trying to find my centre. I was working with sketchy images and memories of *Annie*'s life, trying to figure out who I—Maggie—was. I left my temp work, joining Tom in his tech endeavours. It was easy for me to go along for the ride, trusting in Tom's tech expertise. We were doing something together, which was important to me.

While the business consumed us, we somehow carved out space to contemplate our future, the family we both knew we wanted.

Discussions about children and adoption filled our long drives into the city for work. We constantly questioned whether we were doing the right thing, given our busy work lives. We agreed family was first, and once children came along, I would spend my time raising our tribe. It was something I was keen on. I would be present for our children; I sensed Mother had never been there for *Annie*.

From time to time, I did wonder about my multiplicity. Were the girls hiding away somewhere? Did they sense what was going on? I was met with absolute quiet internally. I could sense nothing and I got lost in the hustle and bustle of running a business and dreaming about our family's future. I started taking the pragmatic approach, opting to leave it all alone. I didn't want to stir up something that was dormant. Why go there when my system obviously didn't want to be known? I hoped this would be an amicable solution, making my life simpler.

Tom was much better at research than I was and would look at the Department of Community Services (DoCS) website, where there was a plethora of information about both in-country and inter-country adoption. Adoption was about the hurry-up and wait, jumping through hurdles and becoming a cog in the bureaucratic system. There would be reams of paperwork to fill out, medical reports to be completed, and the home study, where a social worker would come into our home and evaluate whether we would be good parents. Getting each step of this process done would bring us closer to being parents.

I leaned on Tom during this process. I struggled to focus on the detail, what needed to happen, anxiety getting the better of me, often fearing something would ruin this dream (an unrecognised by-product of my history). But we were doing this together. Tom would break down tasks into achievable chunks, settling my anxious heart, so I didn't feel like I was drowning under the weight and burden of the process.

The first step was requesting an information pack. The letter was thorough, warning us that the approval process, including seminars and case report visits, would take at least a year, if not longer. Then, because we sought inter-country adoption, we would have to complete the paperwork for our country of choice and wait for a child to be matched with us. This could be another two to five years, depending on the country and family profile. It was a long process, but if our goal was to build a family, then understanding and accepting this process was important.

I had heard adoption was hard. This was the reality. Was it any wonder couples often gave up? Between the time and effort required, and what we had heard could be an invasive home study, it was overwhelming. All we wanted was a family. It felt unfair; poked and prodded to prove our worth. The process we saw ourselves heading into would be daunting and demanding.

I would need to master the art of quietly sighing, waiting, and getting on with life. It's what DoCS said. Just get on with life. Get involved in the adoption community. Make yourselves culturally aware of where your potential child might come from. But don't get your hopes up; there were no guarantees. Just get on with life. I did not find this information comforting.

We submitted our Expression of Interest and received notification of our date to attend the all-important Information Seminar. It was then that everything went pear-shaped in our lives. A series of naïve decisions destroyed our business, forcing us to declare bankruptcy. It was humiliating to admit, let alone deal with the fallout. We lost everything—our house, our car—all we had left were the clothes we owned, the food in our pantry and our pets.

But above all, we were stripped of our ability to adopt. For DoCS, financial stability was critical. Providing a child with the security of a roof over their head and food on the table, was of utmost importance. I was terrified as I made a tentative call to DoCS. I made the call alone; Tom was off interviewing for a new job. With a whispered prayer, I dared ask about the importance of our finances in the approval process. The DoCS clerk clearly stated financial stability was a crucial part of providing a secure home for any child placed with us. I knew then I had to discuss the bankruptcy. They were emphatic. This would disqualify us from adopting.

'What about in the future?' I dared to ask. 'What if we worked off our bankruptcy and got it discharged?'

I could hear the quiet at the other end of the phone, and then a carefully worded, 'Once you have your bankruptcy cleared, we would reconsider. But as with any other potential parents, financial requirements have to be met. You would still need to show your ability to provide for the basic needs of a child.'

I mumbled a quiet thank you and gently placed the phone back in its cradle. I remember the overwhelming feeling of grief and loss. The floor seemed to disappear. I grabbed a chair to steady myself. Exhausted, I sat down and cried. I grieved, believing I would never be a mother, never give my child the love and nurture I had missed out on. Desolation consumed my soul.

Over the next few days, Tom and I carefully crafted our email to DoCS, formally withdrawing from the program. We explained our circumstances and looked forward to re-engaging in the process once we had resolved our financial position. My heart shattered when I hit the send button. It felt like a vanishing pipe dream. The reality of having my own family was beyond reach.

In a formal direct note, DoCS confirmed receipt of our letter and welcomed our reapplication upon resolution of our personal circumstances.

Seven years is the length of a standard bankruptcy. I was in my mid-30s. Assuming we were allowed back into the program, age restrictions and the long wait for a child would make it impossible to have a toddler or baby, not to mention multiple children. We would age out of the system. I was heartbroken and spent days grieving as I blamed myself for our circumstances. My past abuse and infertility convinced me we couldn't make our dream of a family come true. It was ludicrous. Trying to find some way to explain away the pain and loss was part of the soul-destroying process of grief.

Tom was ever the optimist. With a gung-ho positive attitude and a barrel of hope, he put together a financial plan to discharge us from our bankruptcy early. Technically, a discharge would permanently erase this financial ruin from our records. It meant it wouldn't come up when we reapplied to adopt.

We were both working ordinary jobs, Tom in contract IT and me as an administration officer. Having lost our home, we were living in a rented house near the train station, with an old car we were afraid to drive for fear it would break down. We scrimped every cent we could and abandoned movies and dinners out. Instead, all our extra money went towards our bankruptcy debt. We hoped the courts would see we had, through fiscal diligence, proven we deserved to be released from this painful and humiliating part of our lives.

We did it in three years. It still felt like an eternity, but our debt was discharged by the time I was 37. It was as close to a fresh start as we were going to get. We might just squeak in under the age limits and be able to adopt after all.

As soon as we received our official letters of discharge from the Bankruptcy Trustee, we requested an application packet from DoCS. With much excitement, trepidation, giddiness and angst, we started the adoption process again. With fingers crossed, we requested, because of my age, to go straight to the application process, rather than attending the Information Seminar. The email stated an emphatic no. We sighed, understanding when they said we needed to be across all the rules and regulations around the adoption process. However, they did acknowledge our age and fast-tracked us, making space for us at the next seminar. I would take any small win I could.

We were hopeful, buoyed by a new perspective and determination to create a family.

For the longest time, I wondered why this happened, why we went through the bankruptcy. There would be a day when I would look back and understand that if the brakes had not been put on our application for those few years, each of our children would not be in our lives. It was timing—they hadn't been born yet. We needed to slow down and wait. No matter how painful the delay, it was our road to each of them.

Origins: My Need

My trauma-filled past craved answers as to the why of my history. Why me? What did I do to deserve the brutality of my childhood? In my more objective moments, I can step back and ask questions about the Parents. It often starts with why they abused me, but invariably, everything coalesces to one simple question: who were they?

This one question drives me. There are so many things I want to know. The truth is, I will never get a complete answer to this question. Even in their death, I imagine their broken hearts over their treatment of me, helping me understand, providing insight into their own histories. Their contrition is a child's fairy tale, an unrequited longing for love. I know this. But it doesn't mean I don't hold a place in my heart where I long to understand why. I am haunted by this longing every day.

Not too long ago I received access to reams of digital information about the Parents. Pictures and enlistment documents make up the bulk of these records. Some from their military careers; when they met, and even their young adult lives when they started a family, living in Harwell, near Oxford, England, where Father worked as a nuclear engineer after the war.

Would this history give me perspective, these snippets of their lives? It was equally intriguing and terrifying. I had lived for so long in semi-denial of their murky influence on my life. But this information, while impossible to prove anything absolute, was my family history. I knew delving into the information on these pages would be the closest I would come to having insight about the Parents. I reminded myself I wanted to understand; I was doing this so I did not revisit their behaviour with my own children.

Birth Mothers

We did what DoCS told us to do. Between waiting and case report updates, we became involved in the adoption community. This would be an important part of our support network. It was painful to watch other couples with their new children while we craved our own. Or hear about allocations and wonder when it would be our turn. But it was also a place where others understood us and accepted our desire for a family. Many of these couples would be a bedrock for us, providing support during the difficult times. They had walked in our shoes and understood.

Parallel to our own adoption journey, any future children we might have were beginning their own painful path of separation from a birth mother who gave everything so they could have a life.

I was gaining a new appreciation of birth mothers. In our Information Seminar put on by DoCS we heard several stories where birth mothers lived under judgement and condemnation, even before their child was born. I believed birth mothers were courageous and determined, desperate to provide for their child, despite the pressure and challenges they faced. Were they going through their own hell, coming to terms with their life circumstances if they kept their child? They would need to do the impossible—raise a child, provide for them and be a mother, all while trying to make their own way in the world. Against all odds, they loved their child and wanted the best for them.

A birth mother's ultimate gift would also be her greatest sacrifice. Their love ran so deep, they would give up their rights to be a mother so that their child might have a better life. The hope of a life free from poverty and judgement drove them.

No quantifiable standard could measure the love of our future children's birth mothers. Each of them simply did the best they could in their circumstances. Theirs were journeys of relinquishment, of letting go of a mother's dream. Their selfless act would place our future children in the very orphanage that identified Tom and me as their ideal parents. It was an intertwined journey of love, loss and acceptance I would keep close to my heart, always.

Origins: Fact or Fiction?

I waded through the Parents' history, from their birth to my birth and beyond, from fighting in WWII to starting a family and following the immigrant dream of moving to a new land, full of promise, hope and a future. What did I learn? Did finishing this research give me something, anything, to create a complete image of what happened to me? Did it give me some sense of satisfaction in knowing the truth of who they were?

There was simply nothing tangible. It was all insinuation and assumption—nothing I could use to draw a line in the sand and say, this, *this is my truth.*

Was it my fault? Letting the things I knew fade to a blurred memory? Was it a product of my dissociation? Probably both. For decades, I made the conscious choice to ignore who the Parents were. At first it was because they were on the other side of the world. And then they were dead. I assumed this would make it easier, giving me the ability to let go. I was fooling myself. The questions, the need to understand. It was all too insatiable.

In therapy, I tried to put a framework around who Mother was. Instead, I found it easier to shy away and move towards the visceral nature of the relationship with Father. I made a not-so-subtle choice to look at what happened with Father, avoiding a deep dive into the mysterious bond existing between mother and child.

I stared for hours at these faded sepia photos of my family, taken long before I was born. Mother's eyes were a snapshot of her history; what was she thinking? What significant things were happening to her? I was engulfed in a web of words refusing to be acknowledged. It was a mental grey fog rolling in like clockwork, stripping my thoughts from me. On the odd occasion where I could find words, they became a list of questions with no answers, leaving me befuddled.

I tried creating a fictional version of the Parents' existence to paint a picture of who they were. I attended a writing workshop on character development, hoping I would learn some new technique to create a compelling story about Mother. The instructor wrote on the board one of Vonnegut's *Sixteen Rules of Writing*. Rule Number Six: *be a sadist. Put your fictional character through hell.* I felt freed, as if I had permission to imagine the worst about Mother.

And with gusto, I created an image of a woman of fiction. A window dresser enamoured with beauty, traversing cobblestone streets on her way to a mundane job. Involved in questionable and risky sexual behaviour in the military and then in a coercively controlled relationship with Father. I imagined all the experiences she had, from her childhood right through to having her boys, then suffering two miscarriages and other losses. She was a woman full of her own resentment and frustration, suffering from her own mental illness, which would ultimately lead to how she treated me. And yet, while it read as a passable short story, it was complete fiction, with no substantive basis to support it. It was a house of cards which, with one breath, could be blown away. This was not something I found satisfying to my soul.

I went back again, looking closely at each image, photo and historical record I had about my family's history. I began considering, pondering, and yes, speculating. Instead of creating a fictional half-truth, I looked for fact in these pictures. Did the truth of my childhood lie somewhere between these two perspectives of truth and fiction?

In the System

We held our breath, letting out an excited exhale when we received our invitation to re-enter the adoption program. First step, the Information Seminar.

For two days, we walked through the adoption process. Little had changed, and the process felt full of government bureaucracy, insisting every step was designed to ensure the best for the children. We took part in gruelling self and group assessments and questionnaires. These activities were meant to help us understand ourselves and our motivation to adopt. Instead, my internal childhood tapes of abuse and MPD rang loud, and I began doubting I was good enough to parent. With what felt like a lead brick strapped to my shoulders, I listened to everything they said, reminding myself this was all about having a family. I tried to combat these fears, telling myself we were dealing with real people who simply had a job to do. I relied heavily on Tom's quiet and considered nature, which helped abate my fear.

An important part of this seminar was the one-on-one session each couple had with a social worker to discuss our dreams and hopes. This would help determine the feasibility of our choices, clarify the process, and refine our perspectives for a smoother transition to the formal adoption process.

The social worker smiled as we sat down with her.

'So, how are you coping with all the information?'

It was a polite way to ease into any issues or problems we might be having. She looked at Tom and then at me.

'Is everything making sense? Where do you see yourselves going for the next part of the application process?'

'We're wanting to go with the inter-country adoption program. The Philippines.' I said with a perky voice.

'Hmmm.' She wrote this down on her information sheet. 'Being pragmatic, you would probably only get approved for the China overseas program,' she said.

She didn't look up, just stated a fact.

I jumped in. 'But we said in our Expression of Interest we wanted to do the Philippines.' My foot tapped quietly in frustration. I assumed they read our paperwork, understood our desire and what I regarded as very rational reasoning behind our choice.

'I just don't see them approving you. You have age against you, and speaking honestly,' she hesitated here, looking at us kindly, 'well, your weight, for both of you, will be an issue. The Philippines program has a very strong bent towards younger, healthier prospective parents.'

Here we go again, I thought to myself. Bigotry based on size. It was a mental burden I carried constantly. I knew my weight issues resulted from a lifetime of protecting myself from abuse. I got it. But this wasn't something I wanted to discuss, especially at this early stage of our application. I could feel my anger rising as I gripped my knee to stop it from bouncing. I reminded myself to remain calm, shelving my anxiety and forcing myself to listen.

'ICAB—the Inter-Country Adoption Board in the Philippines—has some strict regulations about who they will and won't approve. I simply don't think you would come close to qualifying. I don't want you to waste your time or be disappointed.' With each word, I felt our adoption dream slipping away, again.

I responded firmly and politely, knowing I needed to, at the very least, appear to cooperate. 'We meet the infertility requirements.' I said, 'And what about religion? The Philippines is a very religious country and wants families with a strong faith commitment.'

I watched her shake her head as I continued my short but determined diatribe. 'And how about my appreciation of the culture? I've lived there, spent extended time staying with families. Surely it would matter to them for a prospective family to appreciate the Filipino culture?'

She shrugged her shoulders, mentally weighing it all up. 'I dunno. I still think China would be a better option.' She put her hands on the table. 'Look, I don't want to stop you from pursuing your dream. But I think you'll be disappointed. It will delay creating the family you want by being so insistent on the Philippines.'

She paused, weighing up her next words carefully. 'And if I'm truly honest, even for us, you don't meet our criteria. We have strict medical conditions, additional forms for your GP to complete. Your size means we will request a second medical report to affirm your life expectancy and ability to parent because of your weight. DoCS will want a commitment from you to lose weight—because it is in the best interest of any children you might have placed with you. The Philippines is really strict about this too.'

I wanted to scream. Didn't she understand I'd gone through a lifetime of yo-yo dieting trying to appease and prove to others I could control my weight? It had never worked because my ingrained thinking was that fat had been my protector in a home full of abuse. I held my hands in my lap to keep calm; it was obvious they were simply ticking bureaucratic boxes and wouldn't understand. I kept quiet.

Tom could see my frustration and stepped in, speaking calmly when I couldn't. 'We really want to try for the Philippines.'

She nodded. 'Okay. Let's take it one step at a time, yeah? First up, you have to be approved by DoCS. You can't even designate a country until the end of your case report, so let's just take it bit by bit and see where we end up.'

We were at a polite impasse, neither the system nor us giving in, but both willing to move forward cautiously. Internally, I was more determined than ever we would adopt from the Philippines. It felt like the right choice. But as with many parts of this process, I was learning not to voice my frustrations, instead I smiled and nodded in acquiescence.

Honestly? I was terrified someone would discover my history of abuse and MPD diagnosis, even after all this time and distance from my life in the US. My system was quiet, but I knew they were there. It was another way I denied the reality of my life. Shame drove my intense need to hide who I was. Should I draw a line about what I shared? What if some sort of trigger caused my system to come to the forefront? I had spent my early years in Australia denying the ramifications of my young adult life, but I couldn't escape it. Thinking I had boxed up all the anxiety and anger from *Annie*'s young adult life and shoved it away in a corner, I was watching this neat box of crap unravel, keeping it internal, rather than allowing it to consume me the way it had when *Annie* was younger. I imagined a big black mark being slashed through our names if any of my history came out. Irrational? Absolutely. But this is typical for trauma survivors—living with the shame of being found out, constantly hiding who we are.

A cooperative and positive approach was the carrot held out to us. This would ultimately build our family. Remember why you are doing this, they said. Read books about adoption, attachment and issues adoptive families face at various stages. Get involved with the adoption community, hear their stories and develop a network of relationships in which any children we might have would find acceptance.

We were given a stack of paperwork at the end of the DoCS seminar; copious forms and documents would be the bulk of our application. The dreaded medical reports, financials, references and self-assessment questionnaire. Page upon page of our lives exposed. After finishing these, and DoCS acceptance, a social worker would walk us through the home study.

The home study was integral to the DoCS approval process. A social worker would come into our home; lengthy discussions would ensue about our lives and suitability to parent, ensuring our home met dictated safety requirements. We'd heard stories about how invasive this part of the process could be. Nothing was off limits. The social worker came into your home, digging into every facet of your life. Everyone we knew who had been through the process said we just needed to steel ourselves and get through.

I was already terrified, over-analysing every minute detail of what I'd written, or wondering what might trigger my system during the home study. Adding this layer of dread over my history being unearthed by a social worker was stretching my limits of coping. During dinner one night, Tom mentioned I was becoming paranoid. I have no doubt he was right.

Between *Annie*'s life and now mine, we'd spent an entire lifetime hiding our truth. Not the abuse, but the MPD. I was sure if anyone found out, they would think I was crazy. *Annie* had seen a therapist, exposing those dark parts of her life, and felt accepted and safe. Her therapist was there to support her.

The caseworker's job was to see if we passed muster. I had no confidence in DoCS. I believed if I shared intimate details about my life and struggles with MPD, it would further complicate the adoption process. Of course there would be questions. In the self-history section of our application, I was upfront about the abuse, painting a picture of survival and strength, of healing. But I drew a line in the sand with being multiple. I hid this truth, certain revealing my diagnosis would lead to our immediate rejection.

It was *Annie* who had varying success with friends in the past, who had accepted this part of our life. For some, it made no difference. However, there were a few who, when they learned the truth, suddenly felt *Annie* was somehow dangerous. People she trusted betrayed her. This fear lingered. I was now feeling it smouldered deep in my bones. Would the system ultimately judge me too?

Instead of risking exposure, I kept my story simple. My parents abused me. No more. I described how I'd been in therapy for ten years and I was fine now; I had grown and healed. Emphatic this was enough. There was nothing else to wrestle with; I was ready to move on. All true, but a sanitised version of my childhood I hoped would be easier to sell to DoCS.

In retrospect, the rules and stipulations, along with my own perspective on my childhood, coloured my thinking. The rules emphasised safeguarding children and ensuring prospective parents could care for any child placed in their custody. And while for us, and many others who simply wanted to love and nurture a child, the rules felt horrible and demeaning, on a practical level I understood why they were in place.

The enormity of the adoption process is overwhelming for even the most 'perfect' couple, let alone ones like us, who failed several crucial criteria.

DoCS assigned Jane to us for our home-study. She was a by the book, committed to doing everything in a straightforward way social worker. She was thoughtful and measured, even if initially aloof.

Keen to make the best possible first impression, I cleaned the house from top to bottom. It was spotless. No small bit of cat fluff or dog hair could be found anywhere. Counter-tops scrubbed, I convinced myself anything less would deem us unworthy to parent.

This was a common reaction for adoptive parents, especially those who had no biological kids (we didn't understand the concept of having kids equalled a messy home). My desperation to be approved ran deep.

When Jane walked through our front door and into the intimacy of our home, I was terrified. As we sat down at the kitchen table, I pulled out all the hostess stops and offered her morning tea and the drink of her choice.

'Water's fine, thank you,' was her direct response. It felt like she was telepathically saying, *You can't pull the wool over my eyes. Trying to impress me won't win you any brownie points.*

Things would change over the course of our relationship. The more she got to know us, the more she relaxed. She even dared to have a cup of tea when she came to discuss our final report. But I never really overcame my nerves, always wondering if I would slip up and say something to expose my dark truth.

On the first day, she went through the details of what the visit schedule would look like. Provided there are no issues, the report would be done within six months. And then reiterated something always came up to cause a delay, whether because of a hiccup in the paperwork, someone being sick, things beyond anyone's control. She talked briefly about meeting individually with each of us, just to help gauge what our marriage was like and if there were any challenges we might face.

Jane looked directly at me. 'I will want to talk to you in a lot more detail about your history and how you see yourself parenting as a trauma survivor.'

I smiled in compliance, though my heart raced. 'Of course.'

I appreciated this subtle reference to help me steel myself for what was to come. What else could I do? I was already crumbling inside, but I was determined to portray an air of confidence to convince her I was worthy to parent.

The idea of having my trauma history revisited was terrifying. What questions would she ask? Would I have to recount details of my childhood? Why did I need to rehash my history to prove I had healed? No survivor wants to go there. I was no different. I saw no reason to revisit the past. *Annie* had done the therapy. Now it was my turn. I was married and living a fulfilling life. Of course, we'd had our difficulties, but we were here, together. Didn't this speak for something?

Jane gave nothing away on her first visit. 'I'll show myself around if you don't mind, then you can show me the backyard.'

Being dictated to in my own home put me on edge. I did the mental gymnastics required to keep my emotions in check, ensuring we came across in a positive light (heaven forbid my MPD triggers, which came out from time to time, might expose me). Jane's somewhat austere presentation made me feel like she would brook no interference from us in this process.

Tom and I sat in relative silence at the kitchen table while she wandered through each room. His occasional smile and hand squeeze reminded me we were in this together. My mind ran wild, imagining what she might look for. Bare electrical cords? Corners a child might hurt themselves on? My mind was in overdrive wondering if she thought we had some hidden torture chamber.

These were utterly ludicrous thoughts but revealing as to my state of mind. My fear DoCS would not accept us was playing directly into childhood triggers of never being good enough for Mother. They had already pulled us down with the requirements for additional medical reports; I was sure some other flaw was all they needed to justify rejecting us.

Done with the inside, Jane asked us to show her around the backyard. We talked about the play equipment we would purchase and the tree house yet to be built. She said little, wrote notes and took a few photos.

And then, out of the blue, she said. 'Have you thought about the China program? They aren't as picky as the Philippines. It might be a better choice for you?'

Why was this happening again? I took it as a criticism of our qualifications and an implication we set the bar too high. Our goals were too ambitious, our desires unreasonable, and we should settle for whatever solution they presented.

Tom and I looked at each other. He saw the frustration in my eyes and intuitively stepped in. 'Maybe,' he said. 'But let's see how far we can get with the Philippines program before changing.'

I sighed. Tom saved the day, again, knowing how to say the right thing in these moments and ease the tension building in my gut. I wanted to blast her and the entire system. He knew how to play the game and tell them we were amenable.

Jane smiled. 'Sounds like a realistic plan.'

Tom placated DoCS again; he was good at that. I was seething, but refused to let it get the better of me.

When Jane left, we both collapsed on the couch, weary from our encounter. We let the quiet of our home envelope us. With the dogs at our feet demanding attention, we began to unpack the immensity of this process and the weight of the intrusion in our lives. Tom handled it better than I did, his phlegmatic personality ensured this, but even he was overwhelmed.

As for me, I simply couldn't connect the dots between my growing anxiety and a system of alters that I was refusing to acknowledge.

Origins: Examination

In this plethora of information I received, there are stories and moments captured in the information, painting a story of two lives coming together to begin a family. I sat for hours wondering about these photos, where Mother looked like Doris Day—elegant and beautiful—dressed in classic 1940s fashion with a tiny waist and hourglass figure. There are images of Mother and Father in the hostel where they met and served in WWII, both members of the RAF. I read a newspaper clipping featuring a portrait Mother did of Father which she entered in a local art show, a testimony to her innate creative ability.

I also wonder about the lack of evidence, those things missing. Maybe the sources were limited? Could the images have been destroyed by time, lost or forgotten? This was a logical conclusion. It was blatantly obvious there were scant pictures of my birth, and a smattering of other images as a young child (you could count the sum of them on two hands). The bulk of the pictures were of my brothers, playing with dogs or hitting balls, swimming in creeks and laughing. Is the lack of a pictorial tale of me just as much a part of a silent story? Is this a hypothesis I dared to make?

Could this vast array of information allow me to surmise a timeline of who Mother was? Could I weave a story about Mother to help me understand her? It was confronting to consider. I might finally begin to understand this enigmatic figure from our childhood (I reminded myself it was *Annie*'s life)? Would this examination explain the choices she made in her life, and later regarding me? Would it be possible, between historical notes, *Annie's* memories, *The Girls'* experiences and my postcard images, to piecemeal together some sort of understanding of Mother? And, just as importantly, would my story be an accurate reflection of who she was, or a whim and desire of a perspective I was desperate to justify?

I laboured over every small nuance of her life, everything I could pinpoint in the records at hand, trying to find some rational explanation for who she was. If I were honest with myself, I was looking for the why behind her inability to protect me as a child. And even more, was there something I could do to protect my own children from this generational relationship with trauma?

Approved?

I developed tunnel vision. Everything, and I do mean everything, was about our approval. Refresh, refresh. I checked my emails constantly and my phone for messages, desperately hoping someone in the bureaucracy of DoCS would say the magic words: you are approved. I knew I wasn't alone in this. Other couples in the process felt it too. It helped to normalise my tumultuous feelings.

Neither Tom nor I realised, until the paperwork had all been done and the case report submitted, just how exhausting the entire process had been. We collapsed on the lounge in relief when all the visits and reports were done. We had survived the bankruptcy, the humiliation of being told we were too fat. And now, we wanted the golden stamp of approval. It would mean we had jumped through all the hoops and myriads of tests and roadblocks DoCS had put in our path and succeeded. DoCS would deem us good enough to be parents.

I imagined somewhere in the bowels of DoCS those in charge would sit around a large table piled high with files to approve or reject, questioning each couple's viability to parent. After much debate, if we passed muster, someone with a big rubber stamp would receive our file, ink their pad and, with a resounding thunk, stamp the word APPROVED across the front. And then, with much aplomb, we could celebrate our hope for a family.

The reality was quite different. A clerk sat at their desk, verified receipt of all required information, and forwarded it to a section supervisor for final approval. If no issues arose, DoCS wrote a personalised form letter congratulating us on being declared prospective adoptive parents. And, because we had chosen the Philippines program, new application forms for the Philippines were also included. Tom and I celebrated with a day out in the Sydney CBD. We had lunch and then went into a boutique toy store to buy our first stuffed animal, claiming our place as prospective adoptive parents.

This hope of a family gave me some perspective. While I constantly tried to push aside the reality of my MPD life, I could see how it seeped into the entire process. *The Girls* had been told they deserved nothing good, or if anything went wrong, it was what they deserved. What I wanted now was to look forward, to our future family. I continued to push *Annie* and *The Girls* out of my mind when they would find room to wrangle into my conscious thoughts, desperate to prove to myself MPD was irrelevant to my life.

And so began another round of paperwork, this time for approval in the Philippines. It seemed never-ending. How many times did we have to write our name, address and phone number?

This time felt different. We had challenged the system, stood firm in our desires and beliefs, and made it across the DoCS finish line. Tom and I felt invigorated, holding a quiet optimism in our hearts.

The paperwork didn't seem so daunting this time. There were some things we could transfer over, like our referee statements and letters of employment, but others we could not. We had to write about why we wanted to adopt from the Philippines. This wasn't hard; it was simply time-consuming. As always, it was my love for the Filipino people and appreciation of the culture taking centre stage. This, along with my time in the Philippines and our Statement of Faith, was central to our choice of the Philippines. They wanted pictures—us together, our home, our pets—a visual representation of us as the applicants wanting to bring a Filipino child into our lives.

We completed our paperwork with lightning speed, and within months sent our precious package to DoCS. They would be the official channels of communication for us. In no uncertain terms, we should not contact the Inter-Country Adoption Board of the Philippines (ICAB) directly about the status of our application. DoCS would be the go-between, and to do anything different would jeopardise our prospects for adoption. Official communication with ICAB would happen once we had an allocation and arrived in the Philippines. For now, we had to trust DoCS was handling things in a swift and thoughtful manner. Our confirmation email from the country coordinator for the Philippines said they would be sending our paperwork to ICAB. They also stated they lacked control over the ICAB approval process and would update us as much as possible. In other words, don't call us—we'll call you.

I wanted fireworks; I expected them. Lots of hoopla and excitement when we were ICAB approved. It was a momentous experience requiring significant fanfare. Surely DoCS could appreciate how important this was. But no. Several months later, we received a brief email from the clerk responsible for the Philippines program congratulating us and stating we were now prospective parents in the ICAB Adoption Program. The clerk also reminded us an allocation wasn't guaranteed, but we would now be part of a pool of other prospective parents across the globe ICAB would consider on the waiting list.

I knew my perspective was cautious and full of fear, even with the hurdles we'd overcome. I always assumed the worst. Yes, the adoption process was (and is) difficult, and yes, one thing which got us through the wait was having substantial support, both from within and outside of the adoption community. Under it all, I still feared my past would catch up with me somehow, creating problems. Despite my desire for optimism, I worried everything would collapse, leaving us without a child. I couldn't let myself relax, enjoying that Tom and I were well on our way to having our own family.

Origins: Babs

Between the images I hold in my mind, memories from *The Girls,* and comments made by family, I have learned a few things about Mother's life. These stories, along with the pictures I received, interlace to create a more complete portrait of Mother for me.

There is little known about Mother's early life. She was born in November 1925 in the port city of Southampton, on the south coast of England, the youngest of three girls. Her mother married a Scot, a mariner who died in April 1927, when Mother was two. The ancestral history report I have states he died in an isolation hospital in Southampton. These facilities specialised in preventing the spread of highly infectious diseases prevalent in this era; diseases including scarlet fever, diphtheria, tuberculosis, and even the Spanish Flu, still lingering after the 1918 epidemic. These hospitals were often located on the outskirts of towns, having limited medical staff and restricted visitor access. Historians have described the atmosphere created by this particular hospital's stained-glass windows as lovely.

In the only photo of Mother as a child, she is sitting on the grass with her two older sisters. Although the photo is undated, it was likely taken in 1926 because she seems less than a year old. The description includes the girls' names. Mother was called Babs, short for 'baby'.

Is It Any Wonder

During the adoption process, I began thinking about Mother more than I was willing to admit, determined to find a way to explain our relationship in case it came up with our social worker. This clouded history was a trigger for me and *The Girls*.

I would ruminate on the memories *Annie* had and try to find some way to sanitise the narrative in my mind. I was trying to come up with a script of some sort to keep me safe against the questions that might arise from DoCS. Would they see inconsistencies? Could I piecemeal together a story to tell them, stemming the growing angst in my heart?

Instead, all I could think about was what I didn't want to say. How my lack of self-worth had been driven into my soul by Mother's constant reminders of my inadequacies and ugliness. Or how the layers of fat and ever-growing clothes size were a stamp of her disapproval. I was an embarrassment to her; in her eyes I was dumb and ugly. The only thing I did well was play the piano, and she even stole that from me through embarrassment and shame. The memories shared by *The Girls* would come flooding back to me if I wasn't careful. All my child-sized heart had wanted was to make her happy.

As a teenager, when the natural desire was to create her own identity, *Annie* pushed against not only the natural rules of families, but an acceptance of Mother's fallible love.

At a gut level, despite the dissociation—despite having no memory of my past—I knew my inability to love Mother stemmed from *Annie*'s fear of being hurt. Which meant my focus was on how I would answer DoCS's questions to circumvent that pain, not on my actual desire and ability to parent. My thinking was utterly clouded.

Is it any wonder I never imagined myself as a mother? Even when Tom and I kept pushing ahead, getting medicals and references, putting together our financial statements, and having conversations, wondering about what our family would look like, under it all I was sure we would never have a family. We developed supportive friendships with other families in the adoption process. But I continued to doubt, convinced DoCS would see our (my) frailties and judge us. They would label me psychotic, marking the end of our adoption journey. I lacked the confidence, certainly the positive historical reference, to be the sort of mother a child needed.

The cognitive dissonance was, I still hoped. I couldn't deny something sparked in *Annie* when she lived in the Philippines. It was in me too—a small flame, a warm presence. I wondered how this change had happened—from convincing myself I never wanted to parent as a young adult to now trying desperately to please DoCS so I could call a child my own. Was I looking for redemption? Maybe under all the fear and anxiety, there was a spark, a hope of rewriting the inadequacies of my past with my own family.

Origins: Window Dressing

I pick up the threads of Mother's life in 1940 when she was 15. She lived with her family in Lancashire, near Liverpool. Before entering the military, Mother was a window dresser. The only evidence I have of this is her enlistment form, which states, *prior occupation: window dresser*. She was someone who took pretty things—clothes, scarves, bags and shoes—and put them on mannequins in shop windows to entice people to come into the store and purchase something.

What did it mean to be a window dresser during wartime? It would be two years before she enlisted. Was she a window dresser to help fulfil her responsibility, providing for the family? Was it a creative outlet? I have no pictures, no family connections to tell me whether she loved her work or just went through the grind to bring home a pay packet. I suspect the latter, given she was one of three girls. All the sisters would have had to work to provide for the family. She needed a creative eye to put together a window display.

Everything I wonder about this teenage period of her life is conjecture. I accept this. My driving question, under all the speculation, revolves around her love of the creative and of all things beautiful and fashionable.

Her love of art and painting was something she began developing as a teenager. It is clear later in life, so this passion had to begin somewhere. Did a teacher nurture this gift in school? Perhaps her mother also encouraged her in this way. Was she excited after payday to visit her local art store and purchase fresh tubes of paint or pastels for her latest project? Did window dressing fund her blossoming artistic expression?

It leads me to ask: Because she saw me as none of these, was I less valuable? Was I a failure because I was not beautiful and therefore easily set aside? Did this propensity to discard things she didn't find attractive begin when she was young?

Letter Home

It was an ordinary Sunday morning. Tom and I headed off to church, looking forward to seeing friends and gleaning some insight into what the Bible had to say. I was fooling myself. This was anything but a stereotypical Sunday morning. It was Mother's Day. This meant forcing myself to sit through another uncomfortable sermon about loving, respecting and obeying parents. In this case, Mother.

Through years of therapy, *Annie* had confronted her utter disdain for the Parents and struggled with who they were. These feelings were unresolved and something *Annie* and I shared. What I faced now was *Annie*'s justified, and perhaps even righteous, anger at the Parents. This was in utter contrast to the Biblical principles espoused at church. On days like Mother's Day, I simply cowered in my seat, hoping to survive the sermon without being triggered.

Father died. I learned this from my brother. It was a relief both to myself and to my system. But Mother was out there somewhere. Was she as old and frail as I hoped she would be? I held no love in my heart for her (at least none I would admit). I failed on all accounts in this narrow and painful interpretation of what I thought the Bible said about honouring our parents.

The pastor began his sermon. I steeled myself for what I knew would follow. With quiet reflection, as was our pastor's way, he said, 'I want to acknowledge how Mother's Day might be hard for some of you.'

My head snapped up. Instead of trolling through the church bulletin, I became attentive, curious what he would say next.

'For some of you, Mother's Day brings with it memories and triggers of someone who wasn't supportive, loving or nurturing. They may have even abused you.'

I couldn't deny my interest as I listened to him paint a picture of what parents should strive to be for their children. He created an image of loving, supportive parents built around scriptural principles, acknowledging the bare truth of our lives was often far from this ideal image. I felt affirmed, heard and challenged. To have my painful struggles as an abuse survivor acknowledged in a church setting was a breath of fresh air. While Tom and I waited for a call about adopting a child, I reminded myself I needed to become the kind of mother any child entrusted to us deserved, very different from my own past.

After church, I quietly made lunch and contemplated what our pastor had shared. Tom and I did not discuss the sermon; he had an affectionate relationship with his mother and struggled to understand the pain of my history. I kept my feelings to myself.

I juxtaposed myself against memories of Mother, wondering if I would parent differently. Would I worry about my children, always wanting the best for them, thinking about what occupied their lives and thoughts, even as adults? Was Mother this way? Did she ever think about me, even today? Did she wonder if I was happy and healthy? I willed myself to find compassion for her, trying to acknowledge her frailties. It had been decades since *Annie* had confronted her and Father about the abuse, but *Annie* left me with images of the discussion, which had ripped her apart. In the safety of her therapist's office, the Parents had denied everything, even accusing her therapist of planting the idea in her head. I couldn't help but wonder if there was any love left in Mother's heart for me in the decades since the confrontation.

This speculation became a driving need to know if she still thought about me. Over the next few weeks, I became obsessed and did the unthinkable. I sat down and wrote Mother a letter, telling her about my impending motherhood and, because I would want to know my child was alive and well, I wanted to share this news with her. I wanted her to know I was living in Australia, working, and my husband and I were adopting and awaiting the allocation of a child to start our family. Perhaps to protect myself, I clearly stated she should not see this as a letter of reconciliation, rather I was simply choosing to honour her role as my mother and thought she would want to know I was okay. I had no expectation of a relationship, nor did I want one.

Reflecting on this later, I would realise rather objectively, despite my words, in my heart it was an attempt to reconnect. I did not hold the visceral pain of the loss of the relationship in the same way *Annie* did. I held a quiet hope in my heart for something to change.

I had no therapist to help me wrestle with the pros and cons surrounding my motive for this note. Instead, I let the words sit on paper, carefully folded up on the corner of my desk. Did I want to send this? Was this important to me in processing my relationship with Mother? I wasn't sure. I considered it a matter of maturity that I let this note sit, propped up in the back corner of my desk, a daily reminder to wrestle with the validity of the content. Then one day, I put it in an envelope, addressed it and let it sit again.

I was fooling myself into thinking I wanted to maintain my anonymity. I'd done my compassionate duty, letting her know I was okay. I could walk away. Instead, I included a return address.

I knew as I dropped it into the mailbox, I was quietly reaching out to her, hoping this might be a way of mending a mother/daughter bond severed so long ago. As each day passed, I became more acutely aware of this gaping mother wound in my heart. A need to reconnect with this woman who had been lost to me. I denied this, of course. I brushed off the return address, pretending it was simply a habitual oversight. It didn't stop me from wondering whether she would respond.

Within a month, a letter arrived. Much quicker than I expected. There it was. The truth was obvious; I wanted her to respond. I stood staring at this unopened letter, wondering what Pandora's box I had opened. Even the handwriting on the envelope triggered a response. There was an innate familiarity to the large, bold script, slightly uneven and shaky, a visceral reminder of her.

The letter contained a brief paragraph thanking me for letting her know I was okay and how wonderful it would be for us to have a child. And then the next two handwritten pages were full of reflection on Father; on his death and her loss, how wonderful he was and how fortunate she was to have him as her life partner.

I felt myself go numb. No 'I'm sorry for what happened', or an admission of how our relationship had crumbled. Decades-old denial killed any hope festering in my heart. It was all words of defence; adoration of Father and who he was. It was also, therefore, vicariously an absolution of her own guilt and the role she played in my painful childhood. Not just the abuse, but the gaping wound of not having a mother. There was nothing. What I had intended, with naïve hope, to be a bridge-building letter was bent and shaped into her own justification of her life with Father.

There was no hesitation, no moment of regret as I ripped the letter into puzzle sized pieces and shoved it in the trash. I berated myself for hoping, for wanting the impossible. I found more salve in accepting the loss, rather than a wish and a prayer for something that would never be.

My youngest brother told me a few years later Mother had died. It sat, and sometimes still sits, heavy in my gut, like a boulder I can't move. But not with the emotion of grief, but with a stoic acknowledgement that any hope I had of a relationship with her was literally, dead and gone.

Origins: WWII

WWII began in 1939. German air raids were devastating the British landscape by late 1940, leaving deep crevasses of destruction in their wake. The young men and women of Great Britain were coming out in droves, signing up to serve. There was an air of excitement and buzz amongst the young adults to enlist after hearing the rousing speech in 1939 on the wireless by King George VI telling listeners, *A new year is at hand. We cannot tell what it will bring.*

It would have been a pragmatic choice for Mother to become part of the war effort. This feels like a reasonable assumption to make. Between the destruction of the British countryside and the social expectations, she enlisted in the Auxiliary Territorial Services (ATS) on 20 May 1943. She was 17 years old. Both her parents had been in the military (her mother had been a nurse on a military ship in WW1, her father a seaman). Did Mother see this as an exciting way to make a difference? Was it her means of escaping the routine of window dressing? Was this freedom? Did she have dreams and wishes for her future, opportunities which were more than the acceptable, even lauded, goal of the day to be a wife and mother?

Mother started as a draftswoman trainee in the ATS. It is worth mentioning most women who enlisted, worked in factories, joined the Women's Land Army, or worked on farms milking cows and tending crops. It was unacceptable for women to serve on the front line. These were prescriptive jobs, providing for the men going off to war. For Mother to work as a draftswoman showed a skill set the military thought would be valuable. At Malvern, where the Telecommunications Flying Unit (TFU) was based, she worked with scientists and engineers on radar, radio navigation and other sensitive projects. This information speaks clearly about her capabilities. Did the military extrapolate her artistic abilities to draft work? Did she draw plans with precise detail? Was this a steppingstone for her? It makes sense; it would give her a sense of purpose and drive in her job. She was working on critical infrastructure in the war effort. I interpreted this as her demonstrating grit and determination to achieve her goals and dreams, even if they differed from her pure artistic pursuits she favoured before the war. Later in life she would return to this draftsperson skill, working full time for the local council.

Or is there a more complicated side? One where wanton rebellion and women's burgeoning independence were the ideal? There are many notable historical references to the sexual revolution during this era. Public houses closed because soldiers (both men and women) engaged in sexual activities in back rooms. Did Mother embrace the promiscuity the ATS had a reputation for? Was she the one missing curfew because she was out with men, exploring freedoms she never had at home? It somehow felt wrong to paint this image of her; it felt like a false notion of who she could have been. But if I am going to consider who she was, and who she became as a mother, then I have to ask these uncomfortable questions. Even if they leave me with no answers.

Mother's official discharge from military service came on 1 April 1946, almost a year after the war's end. Over the course of her military career, she went from learner draftswoman to level three. Her records note she had model military conduct. A testimonial from her commanding officer stated: *she is of a cheerful disposition, exemplary character, hardworking and industrious and always willing to undertake any work required.*

Mother first met Father at Malvern. I know this from word-of-mouth stories Mother shared; several group photos affirm this. Nothing indicates the intimacy of their relationship. Was it love at first sight? In these photos, I see a young adult woman who took my breath away because of her physical and evident inner beauty. I can't help but think about her resilience, her ability to hope and strive for those beautiful things she desired, even in the midst of war.

Miracle Number One

Tom and I settled in for the long, agonising wait. Sometimes I wondered if an allocation would ever come. We knew it could easily take two years or more, but it didn't stop us hoping, wishing for our magical phone call from DoCS telling us we had an allocation—our child. Work, daydreaming, and a growing circle of friends—either waiting like us or having already adopted children—filled those days and months. We attended seminars about how to care for children with emotional needs because of the trauma and loss they experienced. We socialised with other families, went on camping trips and dinners with other adoptive families, jealously happy when other waiting couples received an allocation.

I would do the maths in my head around when a couple had been ICAB approved and how long they waited. Invariably, it was around two years or more. Just like we'd been told. Each time it happened to other families, I felt momentarily deflated, but also happy for them. Our turn would come. These connections kept our hearts buoyed, making the wait easier.

We were nine months into our waiting room experience when we were called for a file update. It wasn't uncommon, so I thought nothing of it. We'd just sat down to eat dinner when the phone rang. Jake, our case supervisor at DoCS, was on the phone.

He asked us the typical questions. Are you pregnant? *No.* Have your financial circumstances changed? *No.* The penny dropped as I waved frantically at Tom to get his attention. These were the questions they asked before telling you about an allocation.

The rest of the phone call was a blur. We had been allocated a little girl. Her name was Maria. She was almost three years old from a small orphanage in the hills, two hours out of Manila. Jane, our social worker, would call and arrange a meeting as soon as possible. ICAB's expectation was for the paperwork to be signed and processed quickly. Jake offered his heartfelt congratulations and wished us well. I told Tom exactly what Jake had said. We hugged, laughed and shed a few tears of joy. This was really happening—our dream of becoming a family was now real.

This meeting with Jane was full of hope and expectation. There were smiles and excitement as she shared Maria's case report and the ever-important allocation photo. It made her real, seeing dark eyes staring back at us through the photo. Tom cried. I was elated and found it hard to believe something we so desperately wanted was coming true.

Jane told us we were very fortunate because Maria's case report was extensive and thorough. Little information about birth family histories was accessible in many countries. The shame attached to relinquishing a child often causes birth mothers to give up their babies in darkness and despair.

ICAB was meticulous, collating as much information on the child's family of origin as they could, piecing together a history for the adoptive family, painting as thorough a picture as possible. At times, it was impossible to provide a breadth of information. Maria's case report painted a thorough picture, from the birth family's medical history to the sort of personality the child had and developmental milestones. ICAB's goal was to give the adoptive family as much information as possible.

While the case report was in broken English, it gave us immense information about Maria and a window into her precious life. We read about a strong, courageous birth mother who wanted to ensure her child received proper nutrition for optimal health at birth. Maria was placed in a small, new orphanage with facilities equipped to aid children's growth and development.

> Whenever she hears music, she will hold her playmates hands and then forms a circle and dances as she sways her whole body. She waves goodbye to any flying objects such as birds, air plane or helicopter. She is now two years old, when we gave her birthday party, she was overwhelmed with joy seeing her many colored balloons, she dances and screams, turn around and giggling. She is now weighing 109 kg, her head and chest measured 49, 51 cm long and 51 cm abdomen.
>
> She was able to hold her pen and draws line or abstract figures, can climbs swiftly all by herself in a swing. She loves acting as a lady, wears big slippers and putting her small bag on her shoulder. At times seeing her allowing

> swaying her hair and when it covers her face she will remove it as if she is a lady.

As we read this report, it was clear Maria was developing normally, giving us important insights into her upbringing; the way she socialised, played and engaged with her world, all of it. We were overjoyed to know Maria had been well cared for.

The other important person was Maria's birth mother. For me, it was the information we learned about her and her maturity in handling such difficult circumstances that made me want to embrace her too, saying thank you for the privilege of parenting her child.

> As to the daughter she give birth, she personally expressed that she never give her the life she deserves because of her situation. She is young and her income is very small, 3,000 pesos per month, and could not suffice to support her, besides she is not yet emotionally and psychologically ready to parent her and to do the responsibilities of a mother. Even before the birth of her daughter, she already expressed her desire to give her up for adoption to a family who can provide to her needs.

Reading Maria's case report was overwhelming. Her birth mother's strength, immense love, and fervent wish for her child to have a full and happy life amazed Tom and me. Her love was truly sacrificial.

I was in awe of this child who was being entrusted to us. Even as a toddler, Maria was embracing life. We eagerly signed the paperwork saying we would accept this allocation, excited to start the adventure of adding a child to our family.

Origins: Malvern

Mother may have been working locally, possibly still connected with base life post-war, while the British Air Forces of Occupation (BAFO) transferred Father to Germany. There is also a reference indicating she may have been studying art in Malvern while Father was in Germany.

There are two pictures, circa 1948, of Mother in a full-length black dress, one with a jacket on, the other without. She is smiling and happy. In one photo, I see an engagement ring on her wedding finger; her hands are clasped in front of her and she is beaming.

I have stared at these images for hours, wondering about the intimate details of her life, from morning routines and breakfast to nail polish and lipstick. I feel twinges of jealous understanding when I think about her beauty and hourglass figure. Is this what she wanted from me?

Everything I was seeing in these pictures told me a story of a woman who had determination, a work ethic and beauty. I can't help but be in awe of what she did, the work she undertook and the apparent grace she had, even in the midst of war.

There are pictures from the Geraldine Road Hostel in Malvern, group shots of Mother and Father with friends, mates hanging out. In one picture, Father is the only one in military uniform; Mother and the others are in civilian dress.

There is a picture of Mother reclining on a lawn and on the back of the picture she signs off with just their initials: *To G with all my love J.* There is no date, she is in civilian clothes, and this snapshot appears with other photos circa 1948.

Returning

We arrived in Manila on 31 December 2005. Ensconced in our Western hotel in the heart of Manila, we watched New Year's fireworks from our 15th-story window and toasted a new year bringing huge, exciting— and yes, even terrifying—changes. I looked out our window in wonder. I offered a prayer of thanks and then turned inward. *Annie, we're here. It's your dream, our dream. It's coming true.* I hoped she heard me, and could feel some of the excitement coursing through my veins.

DoCS said ICAB had scheduled a meeting on 2 January to meet with Maria at the orphanage. Much to my relief, the orphanage staff offered to pick us up at our hotel, rather than leaving us to navigate the journey into the mountains ourselves. It was one less thing to worry about. Our sole focus could be on meeting Maria.

I imagined this journey up the hill would be a chance for us to talk to staff about the home, about life in the Philippines, our flights—gentle banter to help us acclimate and get to know, or in my case, re-know this country *Annie* had fallen in love with all those years ago.

Smiles and warm greetings met us outside our hotel. Gloria, or Mama G as she was affectionately called, was the orphanage administrator and spoke fairly good English, making our trip easier. What I hadn't expected as part of our journey up the mountain was Maria. As we climbed into our seats, I saw two carers in the back of the van, each with a child on their lap. One of them held Maria. She was laughing and talking with her carer and friend. Oblivious to Tom and me, she was exactly as I imagined—full of life.

I looked at Mama G, dumbstruck. She gave me a gentle sideways smile and then said they had to take the little boy for a doctor's visit, and they brought Maria along to keep him company. And she added, it would give us a chance to come face-to-face with her—a gentle introduction to these strangers who would now be her parents.

On the ride out of Manila and up into the hills, Mama G painted a picture of the orphanage and its outreach work through a preschool they ran, educating orphanage residents and a few children in the community. They also had occasional clinics with medical professionals from around the world, treating not just the children in the orphanage, but the staff, their families and the local community as well.

I kept looking at Maria, trying to memorise every inch of what I saw. Tiny hands playing patty-cake with a carer, big brown eyes smiling and laughing at her friend. Mama G talked about Maria too. I kept stealing glances at her, watching her interactions. A mother's yearning was already building in my heart because I wanted desperately for her to be in my arms. She would occasionally look at me, abruptly hiding her head on the carer's shoulder. I couldn't help but wonder if she recognised Tom and me from the pictures we'd sent over to the orphanage months before.

We moved through the concrete jungle and traffic of Metro Manila, through Antipollo and into the mountain landscape of Rizal. Lush palm and banana trees overtook the landscape. There were houses built on the sides of hills, constructed from bamboo with besser brick fences and corrugated iron roofs. Smaller trikes and jeepneys replaced the roar of the buses and trucks. Eventually, the smog and haze of the city dissipated, and the gentle mountain breezes refreshed us in the heavy humidity. We headed onto the plateau, travelling through small communities, homes situated close to roads where old men sat on porches and women tended the rice drying on mats at the side of the road. With hills rising in the background, all I could see were rice paddies, dotted with farmers stooped over watery fields, planting their next crop. It was a world away from the chaos and noise of Manila.

The familiarity of the landscape triggered a small bout of dissociation, and even sadness. I would tell people I had lived in the Philippines as a young adult, but in truth, it was *Annie*. She had lived here, and I was now vicariously appropriating her memories. Feeling a tinge of guilt, I realised we were living out the fulfilment of her dream to mother a Filipino child.

The Philippines flooded my soul, reminding me what this place meant to *Annie* and her experience with the culture and people when she visited. With her team, *Annie* left Manila and headed to the north of Luzon. They passed community after community where life was uncomplicated and the people gentle and kind. When they stopped, locals would walk through their bus selling refreshments and treats for weary travellers heading up island. Someone had already told them to avoid buying anything unless it was commercially packaged to prevent the dreaded gastro. Westerners were particularly susceptible. Vendors would walk the aisles with juice in plastic bags with straws and sweet sticky treats. They looked delicious but were strictly off limits. Then there was the *balut*. *Annie* peaked over the shoulder of a Filipino sitting in front of her who was preparing to enjoy this delicacy. As she watched the young man peel back the shell, she could see the beak and webbed feet in a gelatinous casing. *Annie* leaned back in her seat. She would not be tasting that.

'We're almost home,' Mama G said, as the van turned left down a small one-lane road, bringing me back from my daydreams. I saw a few *sari-sari* stores attached to homes—the Filipino version of a mini two-dollar shop, selling a variety of goods and concoctions, from tinned sardines, crackers and coke to plastic bowls, buckets and plates, along with fresh bananas, mangoes and rambutan.

The van slowed down in front of a tall, bright forest green iron gate. The gate itself had spikes on top, and as I looked at the wall's expanse down the road, I could see glass shards studding the top of the wall. One of the maintenance team would later tell me this was their security system. Simple, but effective. The driver beeped his horn, and one of the staff opened the gate for us to enter the compound. Kids were running everywhere. Like herding cats, the carers were issuing firm commands, moving the scattering children out of the van's path.

I turned around as I got out of the van, excited for my first real interaction with Maria. But as soon as the carer's feet hit the concrete drive, Maria wiggled free and took off, running and yelling as she greeted friends, bringing the party with her every step of the way.

Origins: Domesticated

The next photos of Mother show her relationship with Father's family. They are in the back laneway behind his mother's house in Barnard Castle, in the North of England. There are pictures of them with his mother and siblings. Mother is holding a cigarette in all these photos. This was before smoking's health hazards were discovered; when it was a fashion statement. These little things reinforce the notion she desired to be beautiful and on trend. Her dress, pose, and smile make her stand out in all these pictures. Mother would smoke off and on for a significant part of her life.

Mother and Father were married on 27 August 1949 at Woodchurch, Birkenhead, Cheshire. This was near her home and family. There are no photos of their wedding; all I have is a picture of a marriage announcement.

What becomes evident is a sudden bent towards the domestic. Several photos show their cottage, and include a shot of Mother sitting at a table, staring at a cookbook. I wonder what she was thinking. Was she terrified at the responsibility of coming up with a new dish each evening, or did she relish the challenge? There is even a picture of her version of Coronation Chicken, done in honour of the crowning of Queen Elizabeth II. Later in life, she would enjoy throwing parties and cooking for guests. Is this where her love of cooking took hold?

Mother seemed to become thoroughly domesticated with her first son in 1951. There are pictures of her smiling and cooing over her healthy, chubby boy. Many smiles abound in these pictures, as well as visits to mam. I can't help but note her serious demeanour in a photo of a visit to see Father's mother and sister. Instead of the carefree laughter and smiles, Mother and Father look quite stern, while Father's sister and mother are doting on their son. Mother's body posture is closed and self-protective, her arms are crossed and hands in fists. This could be as simple as coming to terms with the responsibility of raising a family and a lack of sleep, or was she experiencing some version of postpartum depression, unacknowledged in that era? I hesitate to make any authoritative comments about what this means; it is simply an observation.

One thing obvious is the place Father's mother (affectionately called Mam) takes in the family. Over the years, she would go on numerous holidays and outings with them. Why did she take up such a dominant place in these moments? Was it to help? Did she push herself on Mother? Did she offer a welcome break for a woman overwhelmed by parenting? Being a caring grandmother who noticed how her daughter-in-law was struggling?

Another photo of Mother from 1953 also caught my attention. Gone is the youthful blush; instead, I see a mature woman, relaxed, with the hint of a smile. She is leaning against a tree on what must have been a wintry day, wearing thick gloves, rugged up in layers of sweaters, a coat and a scarf. Her appearance is different. I can see from this photo my droopy eyelids are from her (genetics, what can I say?). There is a softness in this photo I am drawn to.

Her second son arrived in September 1954. Not surprisingly, the first photos are of Mam holding the baby. A plethora of smiling, happy family photos follow this. There is a picture from 1955, when my brother was almost one. I suspect he was a happy baby, because many pictures show him flapping his arms and smiling. Mother holds him as he stands on wobbly feet. He is giggling and laughing; Mother laughs too. There is a kindness in her face when she smiles.

There are numerous pictures of outings with family and friends, playing in creeks and streams. Mother seemed to lose her glamorous edge, becoming something of a country girl with no makeup. Just as suddenly, there is a photo of her at a picnic with pearls around her neck and the latest in fashionable sunglasses. As if she was putting on the skin of her glamorous youth, returning to those memories she held close.

Seaside holidays were the norm, with boys playing and splashing at the beach. There are odd images of Mother in stylish one-piece bathing suits or the obligatory choker of faux pearls. With a gentle nod to her fashion sense, she never shied away from the camera. She was 31 and still maintained a shapely figure, not yet putting on the weight she would carry in later years.

The Language of Love

Staff took our bags away, and Tom and I spent the next hour acting like utter buffoons. We followed Maria around, doing anything we could to engage with her. I felt like a failure, wondering how I had fooled myself into thinking I could parent. My daydreams of easing into mother/daughter intimacy flew out the window.

Mama G, seeing our angst, took us up to the guest quarters, encouraging us to get comfortable. In a little while they would bring up *merienda*, a few toys, and Maria. It would be a gentle way of bringing us together. Tom and I were crossing all our fingers and toes, trusting Mama G knew best.

Maria arrived, glowering at being taken away from her playmates. If a carer hadn't been holding her hand, she would have bolted. Mama G deftly read her dark mood and put on a Barney the Dinosaur video.

'This is one of her favourite shows,' Mama G told me. Maria sat down, watching the TV intently, oblivious to the imminent changes happening in her life. Mama G handed me a toothbrush and clothes. 'This is for her nighttime routine, to spend the night with you.'

'Okay,' was my shocked response. I looked at Maria, then Tom. I guess we had to dive in at some point. Through my nerves, I couldn't deny the excitement of beginning to bond with Maria.

Mama G touched me on the arm. 'You'll be fine. Someone will come up later with dinner.'

It wasn't a question; it was a statement of fact. This was the road we had travelled, and it was time to start the work of bonding with our daughter.

Tom immediately sat on the floor next to Maria, intent on engaging with her and creating a father/daughter bond. It went nowhere; she refused to have anything to do with him. I remembered reading in her case report about her having a big personality. I wondered if this was the other side of her big personality: stubbornness. The show ended far too quickly, and she went straight for the door. Tom picked her up and brought her back to watch another show. She bolted straight back to the door, this time calling out. Then the screams started in earnest. With her back to the door, she slid down and started hitting her head repeatedly against the wooden frame. I was there in a flash, pulling her into my arms.

Maria became completely unhinged and hit me repeatedly. I pulled her arms down, holding her in a firm embrace so she couldn't physically assault me. I sensed her overwhelming fear looming. It made sense, of course. If we'd had days and weeks to adjust, perhaps I would have handled it differently. But we didn't. We were leaving the next day, and I needed to form at least a basic bond with her so we could leave safely. I sat on the floor, gently clasping her in my arms, crooning lullabies and stroking her hair through the continuing screams, desperate to wedge my way into her heart. I was tired. Maria was tired. Eventually, tired won, and she collapsed on my shoulder and slept. Victory! It didn't matter that my body was aching and my legs were numb. This was a small step forward.

Maria woke up and stared at me. Tom brought over a small cup of apple juice. She tentatively took it, wanting to leave my lap. I held her firmly, and she did not resist. Instead, she sat there, drinking and holding on to her cup, staring at me with wary eyes.

Tom tried engaging her, but she would have none of it. What became crystal clear was in the short term, bonding with Tom would be a slow and painful journey. Instead, he became a server of food, the lugger of luggage, and a general dogsbody to allow me time to bond with Maria. He waited patiently. His time would come.

When the staff brought dinner, Maria tried escaping again. When they left, she didn't cry. Watching instead as Tom and I put food out on the table, allowing me to pick her up and put her in the booster seat. What a brave poppet she was! She quietly ate her food, staring in wonder at these creatures who looked different and spoke words to each other she did not understand. We talked to Maria too, hoping our gentle voices would become familiar and safe.

The nighttime routine was easier. Maria seemed to have accepted my presence as a new form of carer, gazing at me intently as I sang, *brush, brush, brush* with each swipe of the toothbrush, getting her ready for bed. Tom and I read her a simple book, focusing on pictures. Getting these small routines in place now was important.

I stayed up watching her fall asleep, singing a few lullabies to calm her soul. She was real. Our life as a family of three had started. I barely slept, instead preferring to watch Maria sleep, exuding a soft, exhausted snore with every breath.

The next morning signalled a monumental shift in our relationship. When Maria woke up, her hair was a mess. She looked like a street urchin with bed hair needing to be tamed. Images of Mother's brutal treatment of me when brushing my hair briefly surfaced. I shook these memories off, focusing on the here and now.

To my delight, I discovered Maria loved having her hair combed. When I pulled out a brush, she came straight over and sat next to me, turning so I could gently stroke her mangled mess into submission, creating a sleek and gorgeous ponytail. I sat back briefly; she didn't move. I pulled a book over from the coffee table. Maria turned, looking at me expectantly. The fear vanished, and in her eyes, I saw curiosity.

And then, magic. I smiled, and out of some deep-seated mother instinct, touched her nose with my finger. She looked at me, tentatively reaching out to touch my face in return. Curious about my glasses, she put her finger on the frame. I smiled; she smiled. We were inseparable.

Over the course of the morning, we wandered the grounds, giving Maria a last opportunity to play with her friends and enjoy this place she knew as home before leaving. She held my hand the whole time, showing us toys, play equipment, and occasionally yelling a phrase at a playmate or two. I'm sure she was treating me like a new toy. I was okay if it meant she let me touch her.

A few of the mamas smiled and gave Maria tearful cuddles. It was a bittersweet moment. These women had been her family, loving her until we came along. It was their job to pour affection into these children and then to let them go. I would forever be grateful to this amazing staff and their generous care.

Mama G came over to see us off. She smiled and said after all the screaming from the previous day; she was worried she'd made the wrong decision to place Maria with us. But seeing us together now, she knew she had made the right choice. Maria, she said, would need a strong mother to bond with, and she could see this happening already.

We were on our own in Manila, with no well-meaning orphanage staff to intervene and help us understand Maria's quirks. Our only scheduled obligation was a visit to ICAB to pick up Maria's Filipino passport and immigration paperwork. Apart from this, we would navigate the next few days ourselves, slowing down to settle into our family routine.

We didn't leave the hotel much in Manila; I suspect I was still terrified Maria would look at me, scream, and take off, and I wouldn't be able to find her. Instead, we opted for the safety valve of the hotel, where Maria could roam the vast room, and where we knew she was safe. Watching Maria play with the Dora doll Tom and I bought for her, I wondered if the new experiences thrust on her overwhelmed her three-year-old mind. We had taken her away from her safe, familiar, and idyllic world. Maria went from bucket showers and rice to bathtubs and breakfast buffets. I would quickly come to understand her resilience and my need for flexibility.

Following the disastrous start at the orphanage, I was eager to learn how to interpret Maria's moods, preventing more outbursts. A bath would be a great way to bond, and I made sure it was perfect: 10 centimetres of inviting lukewarm water. I even brought out the special mermaid bath towel with bright, cheery scalloped edges. I dreamed of wrapping her in it after her laughter, splashing and playing, snuggling to continue our bonding.

While initially curious, as soon as I placed her in the water, she let out screams of desperation at this strange new experience. For a split second, I cooed and told her everything was alright, hoping the tone of my voice would convey security. I cupped the warm water and let it run down her leg. Nope. I quickly placed her on the bathmat, and the crying stopped, returning to me our happy, cheerful child. A sponge bath would be the short-term compromise.

Much to my chagrin, Maria loved anything pink. She had seen me pulling clothes for her out of a small suitcase, rummaging through it herself, squealing in delight as she pulled out a pink track-suit and pink and white beads, a gift sent with us by Tom's mum. Maria brought them to me, dropped them on the bed and began stripping out of the nightshirt I had put her in. I was going to have to find the balance between meeting Maria's needs and managing her wants. But this was all about her getting used to us. Having children, I realised, would teach me to not be so uptight.

Later, Maria perched on the cot set up for her next to the window. From the 19th floor, we had a bird's-eye view of the Manila skyline. With elbows tucked in and her hands under her chin, she watched the nighttime activities: jeepneys and cars, lights blinking, people the size of ants scurrying across streets. I stretched out next to her pint-sized body, listening and smiling as she pointed at the bright lights, saying things in Tagalog I couldn't understand. It didn't matter. She snuggled close to me, drinking in the amazement of this view of a bustling city below. I was smitten.

Two days later, we were making our way through the Ninoy Aquino International Airport for our return flight to Australia. Another cacophony of sight and sound. I was unsure how Maria would react, fearful this assault on her senses might cause another fiasco. I knew we could handle it, but how would all the other passengers see us? A white couple stealing away a beautiful Filipino child in full daylight?

We stood in umpteen lines, checking baggage, getting passports stamped and confirming adoption paperwork. Everything entranced Maria, who experienced it all with a sense of adventure.

A beautiful child, it wasn't surprising people would smile at her. She would smile back, her toy Elmo tucked firmly under her arm, all the while holding my hand. I was her safety. A sense of joy filled my heart knowing Maria trusted me. I was doing something different from Mother; it felt like I was reclaiming a part of my life.

Maria courageously stepped onto the travelator, eyes wide. Giggling ensued as the world moved under her feet. We waited in the crowded boarding area where she flattened her tiny body against the glass, watching the small patches of steam come and go as she breathed in and out. At one point, her arms stretched wide in excitement, watching an airplane taxi by on the tarmac.

Terra firma, Sydney. Tom and I were grateful to be back on Australian soil, the familiarity providing us with our own sense of security. It was a strange feeling walking into our home. We'd left as two adults and now we were coming home as a family of three.

Our dogs and cats greeted us gleefully. We found flowers and a present for Maria on the kitchen counter, a gift from our house sitter. Dad carried the luggage while I held Maria's hand. Eyes wide, she was stepping over a threshold—a new home, a new life. An answer to our prayers, hopes and dreams.

Origins: My Mother

There is a nod to Mother's creative talent in the reams of information I have. A newspaper clipping from 1956 is about an art exhibition she contributed to. Although the article doesn't mention her by name, Mother's picture of Father is front and centre in the photograph. Was this a testament to his striking features and her love for him? It also shows a reminder she still made time for her deep passion for art even with two boys at home (now two and five).

I have many questions about the lack of photos with her own family, even at this stage in their lives. There are unending pictures on Father's side of the family, but only two or three of her family, and those are of her parents, and her as an infant. Why is this? Was there a rift in the family? Was it simply easier to visit with Father's relatives than Mother's?

I have no answer to this, only the question of why. I suspect this observation is something I must take into consideration as part of the larger story of who Mother was. Would a lack of attachment to her family elicit her inability to attach to me?

There is a photo from mid-1960 where Mother is smiling. It is a side-on shot, and she is standing with her boys—my brothers—her hand gently touching her belly. Mother may have been pregnant with me in this photo. Did she know then she was carrying me?

In March 1961, I arrived. Maybe I'm being overly sensitive, but what I notice most is how few pictures there are of me. There is a shot of Mother holding me in a van. She looks tired and dishevelled. A newborn third child and camping holiday would explain this. There is a picture of Father holding me up in the sand, and other shots of me lying on the ground, gurgling, with feet and hands flailing about. One or two more shots of me and then it seems to revert to photos of the boys, their playmates and having fun.

What happened? Page after page of beachside photos, Mother playing in the sand with the boys, Father sleeping in a lounge chair. I am nowhere to be seen. I understand babies sleep and cry—and a third child makes life harder—but there were dozens of pictures of the boys as babies. A minute handful of me. And then I wonder, was I already a disappointment? Mother had previously miscarried two baby girls, so she was desperate for a daughter. Did she expect something different from me? Was I a difficult baby? Was she experiencing postpartum depression? Unable to care for me, was I left alone? These are questions I cannot answer, but by giving them voice, I hope to gain some perspective.

Five pictures show the boys and me dressed in thick sweaters and woolie cardigans, playing with toys and posing for what looks to be

Christmas photos. There is laughter, smiles and big-brotherly love. I close my eyes, willing myself to remember—to feel—these moments in some way. Impossible, of course, but these are the memories of sibling affection I would crave to hold close.

I wanted this vast array of pictorial evidence to help me surmise a timeline of who Mother was. Many things in these images, normal to the naked eye, confronted me because there were no answers. I felt hollow. There was no straight-forward rationale for the why behind Mother's behaviour as I grew up. Could I weave a story, come to terms with a tale about Mother that would make sense? Could it explain the choices she made in her life, and later regarding me? Would it be possible, between historical notes, *Annie*'s memories, *The Girls*' experiences and my postcard images, to piecemeal together some sort of understanding of Mother? And, just as importantly, would my story be an accurate reflection of who she was, or just a whim and desire—a perspective I was desperate to justify?

I am left to imagine she dreamed of a family with boisterous boys and delicate china-doll girls. Did she want feminine cherubs she could dress and show off, a mini version of herself who would turn heads and elicit comments of how beautiful her daughter was, which of course was code for, *aren't you a wonderful mother*.

After this, for the next few years, there are various pictures of the entire extended family. There is one colour photo of Mother holding me. We appear to be travelling on a ferry. As always, she seems tired. I ask myself again, was I a problem child?

Daddy's Little Girl

The process of adjusting to each other was slow and steady. Maria was learning to trust me as I tried anything to interpret her needs through the language barriers of the first few months.

What was not happening was a relationship with Tom. We knew this might happen. Most orphanage staff are women, and certainly not tall white males, which could terrify a new child. The reality of this truth wounded Tom, but he never gave up, taking every opportunity to engage with Maria. We would take walks on mountain trails where she would romp and play with the dogs, running right by Tom, acknowledging him, but never allowing him to touch her. If she needed something, she came to me.

I was on the other side of this quiet battle. Maria was always at my side. Tom was great at doing what he could to help, but it was all behind the scenes. I was getting run down and needed a break. She was a happy child and easy to entertain, but I was her security. What we needed to do was gently expand the trust circle to include Tom.

I needed a break one day, so I told Tom I was going to lie down for half an hour. Putting on a Wiggles video for Maria, I knew she would happily sit on the floor, singing and swaying to the colourful entertainers, I told Tom all he had to do was watch her. She would be okay.

My head had barely touched the pillow when an ear-thundering scream emitted from the living room. I bolted out to see what had happened.

Maria ran to me as I came around the corner, clinging to my leg, enormous eyes full of tears. Tom looked at me with his own gigantic eyes and bellowed, 'She bit me!'

'What did you do?'

'I just tried to pick her up and have her sit on my lap to watch the show!' He looked down at his arm. 'I didn't think she'd do this!'

'I told you just to leave her,' I sighed. No chance of rest for me now.

Maria reached up to me, demanding a cuddle. I gave in, assuring her everything was okay. Content, she plopped back down on the floor and watched the show.

Turning my attention to Tom, he pulled back his hand and showed me a small river of blood. I inspected his wound. Yup—a nice, child-sized chunk had come out of his arm. I cleaned and bandaged it. The only thing really damaged in the end was his ego.

We'd been home for about a month when Kate came to visit. Even across the miles, we always kept in touch, with phone calls and regular emails. Kate had been one of the few people who understood the depth of my anxiety over the adoption process. She knew who I was, who *Annie* was, and loved me still. She encouraged Tom and me, speaking with great pragmatic positivity into the chaos of our hearts during the adoption process, sharing in many of the highs and lows of our journey to Maria. When I read her email saying she wanted to come for a visit, my heart sang.

She'd been once before, when we lived in Western Sydney, knee deep in our tech-business. I had carved out time for her then, galivanting across the NSW countryside, visiting wineries and rekindling our relationship. This was different. This time, she was here to spend time with Maria, with us as a family.

In the weeks leading up to Kate's arrival, I shared all sorts of stories about *Ninang* Kate with Maria (*Ninang* was the Tagalog word for Godmother). It was no wonder that when Kate and I arrived home from the airport, Maria embraced her as part of her life, they read books and played tea together. We took Kate to some of our favourite parks. It was a lovely time, not just for Maria and Tom, but for me as well. Kate was the sister I never had, and the physical, heart-to-heart reconnection with me was as important as her time with Maria.

Kate departed for Canada and we settled into a routine of Tom at work and Maria and I attending swimming lessons, playgroups, and a myriad of other playdates. I was adjusting, but as an older parent, I couldn't deny that it was taking its toll on me. I welcomed Maria's afternoon naps, giving me a time of quiet respite from the joyful chaos that my daughter brought me.

Tom came home from work to find Maria with me in the kitchen, prepping for dinner. She was pulling on my shirt and saying *elow* repeatedly, pointing up. It had been a long day of restless naps and tantrums. I had no patience. My only survival skill was to ignore her. I was on the verge of exhaustion. She was learning a few basic English words, but most of the time I had to interpret her needs based on her actions. Even this wasn't always successful. I was feeling like a failure as a mother because I could not understand her needs.

Tom dropped his bag at the door and came into the kitchen, noting my frazzled state. 'Can I help?'

'If you can figure out what to do with her while I get dinner done, I would really appreciate it.'

Tom looked at Maria with her arms stretched towards the ceiling and went into action. Before she knew it, Tom picked her up and took her straight to a light switch where she gleefully turned it off and on numerous times, not noticing she was in Tom's big white arms. I stared at Tom; he stared at me. Eureka.

'Go for it,' I said.

Tom spent the next 20 minutes carrying Maria around the house, turning all the light switches on and off. This was all it took to create a precious father–daughter bond. From then on, they were inseparable. I sighed. I was happy for Tom, grateful for the help, and delighted our daughter had taken another step in trusting us.

Origins: Father

I close my eyes and I can see Father, tall and menacing with his liquor belly. Salt-and-pepper grey hair slick with oil, tendrils plastered against his forehead. Dark eyebrows above ebony eyes; black, classic 1950s horn-rimmed glasses. Everything about him is dark. I have a hard time seeing him without a three-finger glass of rum in his hands, wandering to and fro in the house, reading his journals or paying bills. His fingers were long and wrinkled. In summer, he would walk around in the humid Texas heat without a shirt on, a burgeoning belly and a smattering of chest hair flecked with grey. In this way, I can hold him in stasis. Frozen in time, a small child's image of a man beyond her understanding—someone she was desperate to love but who utterly terrified her.

I see him differently now, half a century later, after severing the relationship with him, after his death. He is smaller, less imposing. But the memory of him remains dark and menacing. It is impossible for me to wrestle with the effect Mother had on me without at least trying to understand Father. How he became who he was and how his behaviour influenced Mother. I needed a clue to explain his demeanour.

Going through these photos, this still-life representation of Father—how can I not wonder who he was? How he became a nemesis in my life? I find these things hard to write about—the two-sided nature of this man who was my Father. I'd rather label him as an abuser, put everything I know of him in a box, and exile those memories to the darkest recesses of my mind.

I look at images of him as a teenager, an attentive, protective son, a young man serving in the military, a doting father to his own sons. I look at the good things, or at least the normal things, he's done.

I despise them all. Because if I am truly honest, I want to hate this man whose DNA curdles through my arteries and lives in my bones, forever binding me to him.

Daydreaming

Before we brought Maria home, Tom and I knew we wanted more children. We wanted a brother or sister for Maria, maybe more. We also knew there would be a wait. DoCS required a one-year gap before we could put in our next application, so we waited.

But in that waiting, Tom and I talked often about what our family might look like if we adopted a brother or sister for Maria. How would she adapt? Would a sibling threaten her big personality? These were all things we saw as typical issues for any growing family to deal with, so it normalised our concerns. When we re-entered the program, we included Maria in these conversations. We were direct, sharing what we could, in an age-appropriate way, about bringing siblings into her life. She was excited.

'When will my brother or sister be coming?' Was a question I would often get. Her language acquisition had been amazing. Between preschool and books, she was on par with most of her friends.

'I'm not sure, honey. There are people who have to make sure everything is right before we send our paperwork back to the Philippines. Just like we did for you.'

'I want a sister. That'd be fun.'

'You know what?' I would say, stroking her head or touching her gently, 'God will give us the right brother or sister for you and for us.'

'Okay.' And then she'd be off playing. Her four-year-old mind kept it simple; she didn't need to process the more complicated aspects of our journey. We simply let the idea of her being a big sister, or *Ate* (the Tagalog word for big sister), sit gently in her mind so she could begin to process and get used to the idea.

This time, we knew we wanted a sibling group. With a glowing post-placement report from Jane, we took the risk. We knew we would certainly wait longer for a sibling group, but it was the last time we would adopt. It was worth the wait. We submitted our paperwork, stating siblings only, and re-entered the system.

I was nervous, knowing my distress had almost done me in with our first application. I willed myself to believe it would be easier this time. We were more comfortable with Jane, and there would be no information sessions. We had navigated the trials and tribulations the first time. After the home visits, it was pure paper shuffling. *We've done this before* quickly became my mantra to keep calm.

Looking back, I wish I better understood how my nervousness about our approval stemmed from my history of abuse. I had a deep-seated need to be accepted, to be good enough, when as a child I never was. It would have been wise for me to get therapy during our adoption process to help me regain some objectivity, but it wasn't on my radar. I was determined to avoid anything that might even hint at, or could make me—my history—the reason we were rejected. Even having Maria in our lives, and knowing we were doing a good job parenting her, didn't settle me.

Nothing had changed. The fears I had during our first application process returned as soon as we started seriously looking at a second adoption. My fear of judgement took hold and was still at the heart of why I never talked about my MPD with DoCS. I certainly wasn't going to change my story.

I believed others would misunderstand my mental health and brand me a nutcase, which would end our desire to grow our family. We'd had Maria with us for just a year, and our adoption was in the middle of being finalised in the courts. She wasn't legally ours yet. What if this information about my diagnosis came out, and they took Maria away from us? These erratic thoughts were back, plaguing me, playing over and over in my mind.

Trying to have a positive perspective, I mentally boxed up my fears, put them away, and focused on a more positive possibility: having more children.

I daydreamed about the children we hoped for. What were Maria's future siblings doing right now? Were they even born yet? Were they boys or girls? What were their interests? How were their little personalities forming? I could already feel myself falling in love with the idea of who they might be and couldn't wait to know my future children. This daydreaming helped my world slow down; bringing a modicum of peace to my heart.

Origins: Son and Brother

Father loved his mother. Of this, I am sure. Pictures of him as a young adult attest to this truth.

His own father died in March 1930, when Father was barely five. There are portrait pictures of both his mother and father when they were young and in love. He was 24; she was 21. I am particularly drawn to the photo of his father, with his round, kind face. Father, instead, has the chiselled features of his mother. There is one other picture of his father in military uniform, preparing to serve in WWI.

I stare at a photo seeming out of context. The only description is the date it was taken, September 1938. In it, Father is a 14-year-old boy, dour and unhappy, with the typical attitude of a young teenager forced to do something he does not want to do. It is a family portrait. There is a man standing in the centre back of the photo. His looming presence would suggest he was the family patriarch. He is a large, athletic man with broad shoulders, his arms crossed, holding a pipe in one hand. Even from this photo, I am drawn to his presence. On one side is another man and a small girl, unidentified. On the other is Father. His sister, brother, and mother are seated. They look very serious, which I can only assume was the norm for family portraits in the late 1930s. Father is wearing a buttoned-up jacket, white shirt and vest. He stands slightly apart from the group, his hands clasped behind his back as he leans further away. He looks unhappy. Who is this man who looms so tall in this photo? Father never mentioned him; no one ever spoke of him. The only man he ever mentioned was his father. And on the rare occasion his father did come up, it was always followed by the statement: *he died when I was five.*

Who is this man who stands as the family patriarch? I have looked at the genealogy records. There is no listing of a second marriage for his mother. I have many questions. Why was Father so obviously uncomfortable in this photo? Why was this photo kept? What made it important to our family's historical records?

What was this man's relationship to the family? I am left to surmise a scenario. At the very least, this strange man is someone Father did not want to acknowledge (both as a child and later as an adult), yet who was important to his mother. Did this man hold some sort of sway over the family? Was he abusive and controlling? Because Father was the eldest son, did he feel he needed to protect his mother, and as a result clashed with this man, who was, for all I can gather, a stepfather figure in his life? Did Father try to step in and protect his mother, or did he cower in fear, afraid of what this man might do, ashamed of himself?

Does he learn at this impressionable age, what it means to demean women through this man's treatment of his mother? Was Father abused himself? Learning a way of thinking that would echo through his relationship with Mother and our family lineage?

There are numerous images of Father as a young man with his mother, smiling affectionately, his arm protectively around her as a photo is snapped. There are other photos with his siblings too, happy and content. Nothing extraordinary, but honest, loving photos of an adult son who cared for and enjoyed his mother. Both Father and his siblings were proud to do their part for the war effort in WWII. Beautiful portraits of his sister showed her smiling and carefree; genuine and full of affection. To the casual eye, these would seem to be historical photos of a family unit doing their wartime duty.

Managing Multiplicity

We waited eagerly for our second application pack. I was full of anticipation. We were embarking on the process of completing our family.

I heard the postman putt-putt and stop at our mailbox, waiting until I saw his yellow vest moving down the street before heading out to the mailbox. Amongst the other bits of mail was a large white envelope from DoCS. The nerves and the excitement hit. I opened the package and started rifling through the paperwork as I went to the front door, same old forms, financial statements, medical forms. I did note that they included the second form that was required for those of us who did not meet weight requirements and sighed as I walked in the house. Oh well. At least having this second form in hand would speed up the process.

As I stood in the front hallway, I felt myself go numb as I read the title of a new form: *Psychological Evaluation for Proposed Adoptive Parent*. My heart was pounding. The dark cloud of a looming headache descended. I had heard about this new requirement through the adoption community grapevine. But I had put it out of my mind. Now, the reality of the situation began to sink in. I sent Tom an email and told him the application pack had arrived, and we could talk about it after Maria had gone to bed. There was a lot to discuss. I wanted to shit a brick.

I thought back through my deliberate decision to ignore my multiplicity. Over the course of my life in Australia, I made a conscious decision to forget I was multiple. I believed I boxed up my history, my alters, the associated therapy, putting my past in the back of a dark metaphorical closet. Looking back now, it seems ludicrous, but I was doing what people who are multiple do well: I dissociated. Experiencing angst, self-doubt and fear went hand-in-hand with living with my multiplicity, but I didn't consciously tie it to my system of alters. I worked very hard at distancing myself from *The Girls* and *Annie*. I could say the words, Multiple Personality Disorder, I knew this was my life; I knew I/we/this body had suffered horrific abuse as a child, but I believed it didn't matter. All the things I assimilated from *Annie* I shoved aside, choosing to believe it was no longer relevant to my life. I didn't think I needed to acknowledge it.

Why would I? I was bonding well with Maria. Everyone said so, including our social worker. Maria was a bright spark who kept me on my toes. Between preschool and social activities, we lived a full, busy life. I had no room in my thought processes for being multiple. My life was all about Maria.

Each time the angst would rise, or I would question something about how I was parenting, from discipline to routine, I simply put it off to being a new mother. I would tell myself my multiplicity was irrelevant. It didn't cross my mind that under those doubts and feelings, my system of alters was having to adjust to my new life as well. I was so wrapped up in parenting and learning what this motherhood thing was all about, I simply didn't consider my mental health as part of the equation.

I had read somewhere about what it meant for me to be a high-functioning multiple. What this meant was that the host (me) was not at the whim of my alters. When a trigger occurred, my alter wouldn't respond externally. Instead, I would feel their emotions and manage as best I could. Everything about my history was contained, and no one would know I was multiple unless I chose to share it. Which I hadn't. The only person in Australia who knew I lived with MPD was Tom, and given his quiet, introverted nature, he never directly asked how I was coping.

Somehow, it felt like my denial meant it didn't matter. Other stories I read about high-functioning multiples indicated most had a working relationship with their internal system. I didn't. From what I could tell, they were all asleep, just like I had been all those years before. I couldn't sense their presence. I even knew their names and purposes, but it was because of what *Annie* had shared from her time in therapy, not because I innately knew them. For me, it was utter silence. I remained convinced moving to Australia was my fresh start in life.

With this requirement for a psychological evaluation, I questioned everything about how I had coped with the move to Australia, wondering if my denial was finally going to catch up with me. The *what ifs* started. What if an alter came out during this session? What if the psychologist saw right through me? What if I slipped up and said something I shouldn't? What if I said too much about my history of abuse and the psychologist, sensing something, required me to have therapy before adopting again? What if? Panic was my go-to position on many things I couldn't grapple with. I easily grew melancholy, wondering whether I could ever nurture and raise another child, or whether my mental health, and specifically this psychologist's report, would prevent me from ever parenting again.

This is how dissociation works. I remember the angst around having to go to this session, but I don't remember the session. I don't remember the psychologist's face, whether they were male or female, or where their office was. I had no clue which of *The Girls* actually attended the session. Nothing. My angst was so triggering that my system, doing what they knew best, took this experience from me. I do have a vague memory of reading the report and breathing a sigh of relief. Nothing unusual. In fact, the report affirmed my (and Tom's) ability to handle any challenges life would throw at us parenting children, both individually and as a couple. The report did acknowledge my history of abuse, indicating I had done significant healing work and it would not affect my parenting.

One of the other quirks of MPD is the difficulty in diagnosing the condition. The very nature of multiplicity revolves around hiding the truth of my life. As a high-functioning multiple, unless I shared my inner world with a therapist, my multiplicity would likely go unnoticed, being diagnosed instead as anxiety and an inability to wrestle with emotionally challenging issues. It would take a significant trigger for the system to become known. Instinctively, I had pulled the wool over this psychologist's eyes.

I was still multiple. It sat like a rock in my gut, but I breathed a sigh of relief. I was managing. I couldn't deny who I was, but I was at least confident I could love and parent my children.

Origins: Warrior

Father was a dapper, striking RAF officer in his uniform. He had dark features and an impish smile, his ears sticking out just enough to add to his physical appeal. There are pictures of him standing proudly with his brother, both in uniform, ready to serve King and Country.

I am surprised at the extent of pictures from his years in service, mostly because it was an aspect of his life he never spoke about. Or how he and Mother met and served together in the RAF.

It was Mother who would talk, on rare occasions, about the German Blitz, hiding in air-raid shelters. As a small child, I found this fascinating. When our family moved to Texas, the US was still zealous over the threats from the Cuban Missile Crisis in 1962, when the world held its collective breath, wondering if we were heading into another world war. Five years on, as students, we were still being drilled to hide under desks at school.

It was Mother who talked about their history in England and the unending German air raids sending them to the safety of shelters.

She reminded us to practice what the teachers had taught us; it was how we would be safe. She always reminded us she spoke from personal experience.

Father would sit quietly, never discussing the war. What I would learn about his warrior life would be gleaned from these photos.

He was a corporal, working as a radio mechanic on fighters and bombers. His records show he was an accounts clerk before entering the RAF in December 1942. There are a few pictures of him on ladders reaching inside Spitfire engine housings or standing in the pilot seat of these aircraft, making repairs.

The photos I linger over show his social life in the RAF. There are pictures of him and Mother, along with a gaggle of friends. Pubs and picnics seem to feature in their time off, with many pints consumed on a regular basis. He already appeared to be a heavy drinker, often enjoying a beer or a stiff drink. This was a theme I would see repeatedly.

In these early photos with Mother and his friends, I see no devastation from the German Blitzkrieg in England, even though the airbase he served at was in the direct line of fire. Apart from the uniforms, you would think they were an ordinary group of young adults out having fun.

Postwar is when I notice a difference in the pictures. He goes from being a man who was proud of doing his duty to a tired, reckless soldier who was done with the war. In 1946, they transferred him to BAFO for reclamation work in Germany. Stationed primarily in Achum, Buckberg and Hamburg, he was part of a crew helping rebuild infrastructure, ensuring the safety of the villages and towns, clearing old ordinances and making repairs where possible. Convoys of trucks became half garbage trucks and half repair stations, moving across the German countryside. Picture after picture showed gutted bombers with swastikas plastered on the sides and damaged ham radio towers. There is one picture of Father sitting on an unexploded bomb. The description on the back states simply, *Ego?* Father's daredevil (or rash?) side must have been coming out. Father was part of a team tasked with repairing equipment as part of the cleanup of Germany. There is a picture of him sitting in a small gun carrier with three other soldiers. The back reads *French gun carrier to ferry comms gear to Typhoons.*

There are images of buildings in ruins, trees black and bare from the bomb blasts. Landscapes full of rubble contained a bare spire or tower standing in effigy to some corner store or cathedral.

I suspect these soldiers served as a type of practical ambassador to the locals. There is one picture where Father stands in front of ruins and the picture states, *1946 Hamburg in ruins, took a #6 tram to the suburbs to see how people live.* There are several pictures of Father and his comrades hanging out with local children, playing games of cricket in cleared streets with nothing but burnt buildings on either side. Father became friends with a German couple who had two young girls. There are several shots, some playful, some formal. In one picture, the back reads, *New Year's Day 1947.* He had formed enough of a bond with this family to spend a holiday with them.

The Malcolm Club was a term used loosely during the war to reference a building in the local area set up as a pub, or club, where the soldiers could go for social respite. These clubs had a reputation for heavy drinking. Perhaps this was part of Father's continuing descent into alcoholism and the escape it provided from the devastation and death surrounding him during the war.

The most profound thing for me to stumble across was a copy of a letter written by a Mr Skeffington, Parliamentary Private Secretary, to Whitehall in London, home to numerous government wartime officials. The correspondence was about the Liberty Train, code-named Operation "Swallow", full of refugees coming out of Poland. Many had died along the way; others had frostbite requiring amputation. There are several pictures of the train, of Father and other soldiers, but not of refugees. It is obvious from the pictures this is something Father was involved with, but to what extent I do not know.

I can only imagine the emotional impact this would have had. To see the devastation and reality of war, lives lost, families destroyed, homes in ruins. Witnessing this firsthand, from the Liberty Train to the towns, would have created immense turmoil for any soldier. The emotional conflict of knowing you had been a willing participant in the destruction of these lives, simply because you were doing your duty, had to be overwhelming. The reality of this commitment would take on a whole new meaning. It would be difficult for a soldier's mind to process this horror without becoming cold and stoic.

The noted absence in all these postwar pictures is Mother. I know they were apart, but Mother's photos indicate constant letters and pictures expressing her love for Father. In this snapshot rendition of Father's military life, it is as if she does not exist.

Wondering About You

We ticked the boxes, filled out the forms—the financial, medical, and psychological reports—we were back in the system again. Jane was back for another round of home studies.

The anxiety had fairly well abated regarding the home study. Jane had seen us in our post-placement visits with Maria; seen first-hand what a live-wire Maria could be. Jane talked and played with Maria to see how she was adjusting to life in Australia. Maria showed Jane her room, her favourite books and toys, and talked non-stop about her friends. Our daughter demanded full attention and engagement. No half-hearted *aren't you lovely, dear* comments while the adults were trying to have their own conversation. She wanted to be at the centre of it all. It was cute and endearing in the short term, but how would she go with a brother or sister who stole centre stage from time to time?

And then we dropped the bombshell. We wanted a sibling group. We always wanted more than two; it was a cornerstone for how Tom and I imagined we would build our family. Finally, we could talk honestly with Jane about this and the impact it would have on our family. Pragmatically, we knew the demands on us would increase exponentially.

This began a serious discussion about how we would handle the fallout. Maria had been queen bee at the orphanage; she was one of 20 children and a standout leader. We would have to affirm her role as a big sister, *Ate*, so she didn't feel left out. We would multiply everything by two or three—costs for groceries, clothes, school; time and how to invest emotionally in the kids, both as a family and individually. Having had the discussion ourselves made it easier to share with Jane. She could see we hadn't leapt blindly into this, but had thought it through, including Maria's need for extended family and belonging.

And there was the wait, the ever-looming time factor. ICAB had strict regulations about age differences between children and how old adoptive parents could be. My age remained a factor. Our window for younger children was quite narrow. We could wait years for an allocation, maybe even four or five. There was a strong possibility they wouldn't be infants, but preschool age or older. Sibling groups rarely became available. These were the pragmatics we had to consider. In the end, it was a productive discussion, and Jane assured us she would write a positive report and case for us to adopt siblings.

We sailed through the DoCS process, being approved within a month. I could feel my heart settle, between these small wins and familiarity with the process, I was feeling quietly confident. Now we waited for the ICAB approval.

I began trolling the internet, looking at pictures on orphanage websites. There were numerous orphanages across the Philippines, most with some sort of American attachment, whether because funding came from the US or the director was American. Australians built and ran Maria's orphanage (I suspect this was part of their reason for choosing us for Maria). I also knew our future children would never come from this orphanage. ICAB rigidly enforced this policy regarding families adopting from the same orphanage. It was complicated, political and emotional. When families adopted, they naturally became involved in supporting the home their child came from, whether by financial gifts or volunteering. It was often done, which was fantastic, but could set up a quiet bias on the orphanage's part for a family they already knew. Fair enough. But it didn't stop me from looking at photos from Maria's orphanage. I saw two beautiful boys with dark, sombre eyes. My heart leapt. I showed the image to Tom.

'Tom, look at these boys. Aren't they beautiful? Wouldn't it be lovely to be considered for them?'

He wandered over and looked over my shoulder. 'Yep, they are. But they're from Maria's home. That'll never happen.'

'Yeah, I know. But my goodness,' I sighed. I couldn't take my eyes off these two boys, noticing while they had soulful eyes, they both had a gentle grin of contentedness on their faces. I knew I had to let the dream go. Instead, I prayed God's best for them and moved on, knowing their home would be elsewhere.

But I couldn't get them out of my heart. The website never mentioned names or their status at the home. For all we knew, the staff may have been working towards a family reconciliation, something which rightly had to be investigated before recommending adoption.

The best thing I could do was to pray for their well-being and God's protection. I prayed for their birth families, wanting whatever would be God's best for these two cherubs. I couldn't help wondering what their personalities were like and if they would get along with Maria. But I reminded myself that this was impossible. ICAB would never allow their placement with us.

I continued to look at images of siblings on the internet. There were groups of two, three and more. I wondered whether my desire for a big family was foolish. Who was I to think I could parent four or five children? It was a naïve thought on my part, but my heart grew hopeful, believing our family would grow.

I looked at a myriad of orphanage websites across the Philippines, places I knew had excellent reputations for quality childcare. I passed the months this way, dreaming and wondering where our future children lived and what they were doing.

To relieve my anxiety about the process, I would often stop and pray for the nameless children I would see. I prayed for their safety and for time to be gracious so their forever families would come soon. I also prayed for us, for our own future children, hoping we wouldn't have to wait long to hold them in our arms.

An email from DoCS arrived unexpectedly, announcing our ICAB approval for a second adoption. Compared with our first time through the process, this was extremely fast.

We stopped all communication with Maria's orphanage, no more care packages or donations. It was the right thing to do, keeping everything open and politically correct.

But it didn't stop me from occasionally looking at the picture of these two boys on their website, wondering about the truth of their lives, where they were in the adoption process, and what activities filled their days.

We became potential parents in the proverbial waiting room again. But this time, we waited, knowing it would be years before our family was complete. We accepted this as the ramifications of our desire for siblings and got on with our lives.

Origins: Family Man

Father and Mother were married in August 1949. There are no records or pictures celebrating this event. Which is interesting, given there are pictures of wedding invitations and photos of both of Father's siblings' weddings. It could simply be an oversight, but for my investigation, this information is missing.

After the Parents were married, Father took a job as a nuclear engineer at the Atomic Energy Research Establishment in Harwell, near Oxford. His job focused on the research and development of weapons, including designing and building nuclear reactors. Historical records of the time show he may have worked on an array of technologies, from medical applications to nuclear propulsion systems for ships and submarines.

It was during his time at Harwell that Father would meet and become friends with Stanley Peters, the man who would eventually encourage Father to move to the States and take up a position at the University of Texas. The Peters family would live near us just outside of Austin. This relationship opened doors, introducing Father to the world of paedophilia. I wondered how much of Father's experience with the man in the family portrait had aided in pushing him towards this deviance.

Life in Harwell appeared to be idyllic. Postcards showed business trips Father would take, with affectionate messages on the back referencing his love for Mother.

Father was a proud family man with two sons. Mam remained a mainstay in their lives, an ever-present familial link. Holidays with Mother and my brothers always involved walks along rocky English beaches, where she would hold the boys' hands, laughing and playing. She cared for them, holding them with a special grandmother's affection. She was a welcome visitor, lounging comfortably in their yard or caring for her grandsons.

I arrived in March 1961. There is a photo of Father in his typical pose, standing me up in the sand at the beach, as if willing me to walk. It is the only picture I have of him with me. His face is not lit well, but he seems to smile.

There are no photos of me with my grandmother. My only memory of her is of an old woman I stayed with as a teenager when I travelled to England. She said I was growing into a *big girl*—code word for fat. I have no affection in my heart for her.

I want to see more pictures of Father with me. Why? If he had bonded with me as a baby, would he have loved me? I see many pictures of him relaxing at the beach; even in these photos, he becomes distant. They are more about him, not about him and his boys. I suppose boys grow, and they want to play more independently; I understand. But the why remains.

And then, just as quickly, in early 1964, we moved to America. Father had secured a position at the University of Texas in their Nuclear Engineering Department. We would travel by boat from Antwerp to Houston.

After this, my life would change forever. But of course, there are no photos of this. There is no physical, solid evidence clearly identifying this man as my abuser. A stranger would not see it. I have only speculation. A patriarchal figure standing as a dark shadow in his youth, a propensity for heavy drinking, a preference for his sons over his daughter—all clues, all possibilities. But nothing concrete. It leaves me hollow, adrift in wonder and confusion, perhaps even angry at myself for hoping this exploration of who he was would provide solid answers. Instead, I am left with conjecture and frustration.

Miracle Number Two

Tom and I settled in for the long wait, we knew it could be five years, maybe more. I would be lying if I didn't admit I sometimes wondered if we'd made a mistake, saying siblings only. Maria was getting older, more settled as an only child. Would this make the adjustment of siblings harder for her? And what about my age? I wasn't getting any younger. My body's groans and creaks were a not-so-subtle reminder I wasn't as young as I used to be. These were all thoughts I had as we crossed the magical one-year mark since ICAB had approved our file. We were doing what we could to pass the time as a threesome. Maria was a joy, and my heart was full.

It was early April 2009 we travelled to Perth, meeting up with other families in Australia who had adopted from the same orphanage. This was an exciting and important trek. As adoptive parents, we wanted to build memories for our kids, many of whom had known each other when they lived at the orphanage. It was a salve to our hearts to watch them chatter and play as we wandered the streets of Perth, or on the ferry for a day trip to Rottenest Island, where the kids gleefully fed the friendly quokkas. These moments together were a positive reminder of the Philippines, and the place their first home had in their hearts.

I was in the habit of keeping my phone close at hand, which was quite uncharacteristic of me, given my general loathing of technology. I was doing what every prospective parent did—wishing the next call would be *the* call. We were in our hotel room, getting ready to meet up with everyone for dinner at a local Filipino restaurant. I was putting on my shoes, watching Tom and Maria playing on the other side of the room when the phone rang. A Sydney number.

I put a finger in my ear to block out their banter. 'Hello?'

'Is this Maggie Walters?'

'Yes, it is.'

'This is Carol from DoCS. We wanted to do a file update. Do you have a minute?'

My heart raced. Could it be?

'Sure.' I walked to the corner of the room to make sure I could hear every word she said.

'I just need to confirm a few details. You aren't pregnant?'

'No, definitely not.' The smile was creeping into my voice.

'Are you both still working? Your financial circumstances haven't changed at all?'

'We're both in the same jobs.'

A brief pause. 'Well, then I'm happy to let you know you've received an allocation from ICAB.'

I took a breath as she continued. 'A sibling group of two boys.'

'Oh, my.'

We discussed meeting with the social worker. I told her we were on holiday in Perth and would be in touch as soon as we were back. She congratulated us and reminded me ICAB required expedited acceptance, so please contact them as soon as possible. I thanked Carol for her time and hung up the phone.

I was stunned, watching Maria play and dance. Her world, our world, had, in an instant, changed forever. It took me a minute to soak in the reality of our situation. Tom and Maria were oblivious.

Then Tom saw my face. 'Who was that?'

I was still staring at the phone, and then said the magic words, 'DoCS.'

Tom's eyes went wide. 'Really?' Pregnant pause, 'Is it?'

'Yeah. It is. Two boys.'

'Oh, wow.' Tom was articulating just how I felt, dumbstruck.

I invited Maria to come over and sit on the bed with Tom and me, patting the bed between us. We told her she was officially an *Ate*, the big sister to two younger brothers. Her questions were straightforward and pragmatic 6-year-old thoughts.

'How old are they?'

'Two and four.'

'What do they like to play with?'

'I don't know.'

'When will I get to meet them?'

'Well, as soon as we are back from this trip, we'll have lots of paperwork to fill out to make everything official. Then Jane will talk to us and bring a picture of the boys and something called a case report so we can find out more about them. But once that's all done, we'll travel to the Philippines and pick them up. You remember Jane? How she came and visited us and spent time with you?'

'She's nice.'

'Yes, she is. So, once we've met with Jane, we'll tell you everything we can about your brothers.'

'Okay!' And off she went. It was all her mind needed at the moment.

We shared our news with our friends at dinner. It was a celebration, with others who had been on the same journey and knew exactly how we were feeling. Everyone was excited with us. These two boys completed our family. My mind was racing at all the planning we would have to do, and more importantly, who were these little boys who were now my sons?

Jane was all smiles when we met her the following week. She shook her head. 'This is truly astounding.'

'What?' I asked as she handed us the case report.

'Siblings. They never happen this fast.'

Tom and I smiled at each other. 'We believe in the power of prayer,' I said.

Jane passed us the picture of these two gorgeous cherubic faces. It was them, the boys I'd fallen in love with on the orphanage website over a year before. Tom and I looked at each other briefly, in awe. I stared at the picture for a minute and then exhaled a slow sigh of contentment. There had always been a candle in my heart for them.

It was on to the business at hand—poring over the case report, wrapping our heads around their story. We shed tears for their birth mother and learning about her difficult family situation and even harder choice to relinquish her boys. The orphanage admitted the boys a year earlier when they were one and three years old, according to the case report.

Kyle was the older brother. He was quiet and reflective. The report described him as very considered and deliberate both in his play and at preschool. He seldom talked or played with others and was already showing a quiet propensity for learning and achieving as a diligent student.

> Kyle, at two years and 11 months, he enjoys playing puzzles. He can name the people around him. He likes book and can name some pictures in it like flowers, cars, animals and others. Before, Kyle was always alone. At 3 years and 6 months old he learned to interact with the people around him and can express his feelings. He laughs when happy and cries when sad, unlike before that he choose to be silent. Kyle is very good at puzzles. He can complete complicated one. He can count 1 to 10 but not yet on one-to-one correspondence. He likes to paint and manipulate colors.

Then we read about Danny. More of an extrovert than Kyle, and certainly socially well-adjusted with those he trusted. Danny's loyalty came through in his fierce protection of his brother.

> As for Danny. He is very charming and accommodating to his caregivers or other adults familiar to him. He loves to kiss and hug them. But on strangers and visitors he seldom sees, he cries when picked-up. Danny is brave and fought those who hurt him. He is also protective of his brother. Once, Kyle was being hit by

> other toddler, when Danny saw what happened, he hit the kid who hurt Kyle and patted the back of his brother.

I smiled as I read stories of how attached the boys were. Danny was, in fact, Kyle's protector, even though he was younger. Danny was a boofy, boisterous boy who fiercely defended his gentle big brother from the jibes and bullying of some of the other children. He was always on the lookout, protecting the thread of connection siblings have.

How would this translate to their lives with us? How would they go with Maria, their big sister? Would Danny watch out for her the way he did for Kyle? Or, I wondered, how would they take having a big sister who looked out for them? Would they see this as controlling? These were all part of our thought process as we contemplated how our family would look, and what adjustments we needed to make.

I reflected briefly on my own relationship with my brothers, severed when I broke off communication with the Parents decades before. It was something I longingly regretted—the emotional, and now physical, distance between us. I wanted so much more for our children.

I stared at their picture again. Kyle and Danny had changed slightly since I'd seen them over a year before on the orphanage website. The sadness in their eyes had abated, replaced by a reflective gaze. They seemed settled, and I hoped, at peace.

In the end, 18 months after our initial approval by ICAB, we received our allocation. Danny and Kyle were our second miracle.

We believed in our hearts a sibling group was right for our family. Our hearts were full.

We immediately began preparing our home and hearts for the boys; going back to IKEA, purchasing beds and toys, painting the room an appropriate boy-friendly gold colour. Doing everything possible to ensure the bedroom we created for Kyle and Danny was safe and cozy. Clothes shopping was a novel experience. With Maria there was significant creative freedom. And while I did what I could to ensure the boys had fun clothes, the options were practical and limited.

At the same time, the boys were busily being prepared for their departure. I wondered if they had received the clothes we sent (cute koalas and kangaroos on adorable pint-sized t-shirts) or if they had seen photos we sent, images of their new room, their sister, us and our pets. I knew too the orphanage staff had to get medical checks done and then passports completed—all little steps as we waited for our official *Authority to Travel*.

My nerves kicked in as the weeks rolled by with no updates on their immigration status. DoCS was hands-off. Don't call us; we'll call you. I understood they were busy, but couldn't help wondering if they'd forgotten about us. These were irrational thoughts; DoCS always gave priority to bringing together families when an allocation had been made. Why weren't they calling us? We'd waited a long time. Had something gone wrong? I noted my anxiety was ramping up, wondering if this was a trigger for something internal. Was the lack of control over our current circumstances something which haunted *Annie* and *The Girls* at every turn? Was this lack of control ramping up my paranoia? As per usual, I shelved it; I didn't have the brain space or practical support to wrestle with this conundrum, preferring to live in the present.

And then, a call from our caseworker.

'I just wanted to give you an update on how things were going. I know it's been a while.'

'Yeah, I was wondering.' Simple words, using them to help me remain calm. Heaven forbid they should have an irrational mother to deal with.

'Well, it looks like there have been a few hiccups.' And then, as if to calm an expected fear on my part, 'But there is nothing to worry about.'

'What happened?' My voice quivered slightly.

'So, from the latest email, it looks like the youngest, Danny, has been sick. Nothing major, just a flu. But his temperature spiked, and they wanted to make sure he was healthy before they took him in for his medical.'

'Makes sense.'

'From what I can tell in ICAB's report, the exam revealed Danny's exposure to TB.'

'Really? Tuberculosis?'

'Yeah. Not uncommon in the Philippines, but the Australian Health Department just wants to check out all the background and facts before giving clearance.'

My heart sank. In my head, I worked through the schedule in my head. My self-imposed rigid time frames were being stretched thin. I had plans to visit extended family, holidays and bonding time already mapped out. 'So, they haven't cleared their medicals yet?'

'No, they haven't. But just because he's been exposed, doesn't mean he has it.'

I could feel the next question rising in my throat like bile. 'Could this mean they won't get cleared?'

This was when a caseworker earned their keep. Most days, they shovelled paperwork. But at this moment, they became a hand-holder and a friend. 'I would really encourage you not to worry about it. It's out of our hands.'

'Have they denied entry to children before? A sick child?'

A sigh. 'Yes, this has happened before with other countries. But remember, they aren't saying Danny has TB, just that he's been exposed.'

'What might happen next?'

'I honestly don't know. But really, I don't think you should worry. Let's just take it a day at a time and let it all work itself out.'

'Okay.'

'Sit tight. We'll be in touch as soon as we know something.'

I would be lying if I didn't admit my anxiety and stereotypical *everything seemed to go wrong* attitude got the better of me. Distress and any related irrational fears were my go-to when I thought things were falling apart. I was terrified something would rip our family in pieces, leaving my boys without parents to love them, forcing them to grow up in an institution providing for their needs, but ultimately, wasn't family.

Between endless pacing and staring at the phone, willing someone to call with an update, the days seemed to drag on. Looking constantly for a missed call or to see if my phone was on silent. Double checking everything. I had to be ready, available when DoCS did call. Each tick of the clock was a moment I wasn't with them. What if the system failed, vanquishing my growing love for my boys?

I began reflecting on *Annie*'s childhood. All those times when she was desperate for the love of her Mother. I could see it all in my mind, postcard images of situations where *Annie* desperately wanted love from a mother who was incapable of loving her.

And now, finally, with my own family, I could give these boys my love. If my boys were taken from me, would I be able to love again? I even contemplated how Mother had felt, wondering if she had wrestled with anxiety and loss after her miscarriages. Or if, when she gave *Annie* over to Father, did she numb herself to the pain of her betrayal? Mitigating her own sense of loss and failure?

My anxiety was building a cyclonic world of its own around losing this allocation. Had we been too arrogant, too demanding when we said siblings only? Despite all the logic and rationale we initially used to say siblings only, I couldn't help but wonder if it was all a mistake. What I didn't realise yet was this was a mother's love. I'd not met them face-to-face yet, but they already held a precious place in my heart.

After three agonising weeks of wondering and fear, I got another phone call. They had cleared Danny for immigration, with one caveat—he would need to have a physical exam here in Australia, within six months of arrival, to confirm he showed no signs of being a TB carrier. I felt a wave of relief cascade over me, wiping away all the tears, fears and doubts. I sent Tom an email immediately to alleviate his own fears.

Within a week, the boys had all their clearances, and we received our *Authority to Travel*, our official invitation from the Philippine Government to return, meet our boys and complete our family.

Origins: Seafarers

There is a photo of a newspaper clipping. I cannot tell which paper, but I suspect it is a regional paper from Father's hometown, or perhaps Harwell. I have omitted the names for privacy. A blurry headshot of Father accompanies the article.

Texas Post for Barnard Castle Man

> Thirty-nine years old Harwell Scientist _____ of Barnard Castle, leave Britain with his family on January 29 to take up research work at the accelerator laboratory of the University of Texas.
>
> Travelling by cargo boat from Antwerp, Mr and Mrs _____ and their young family of three will be at sea for 17 days, a journey which takes them via the Gulf of Mexico to Houston. From there, they and their luggage will be transported to the town of Austin.

> Mr_____ a former pupil at Barnard Castle School, served in the RAF as a radio mechanic during the last war. After demobilisation, he worked at the Malvern Technical Research Establishment for about a year before going to Harwell where he has worked on research for the past 15 years.
>
> As a senior electronics officer at Harwell, Mr _____ has presented several theses which have attracted the attention of scientists at home and in the United States, Sweden and behind the Iron Curtain.
>
> His wife _____ is a keen painter having studied art at Malvern where she met her husband.

There are photos of luggage tags. The front providing their names *c/o University of Texas, Austin Texas. Via Antwerp and Houston. M.V. Woltersum*. On the back it says *Wanted on Voyage*. The note going with this image states: *We take a trip on a ship*! Showing the excitement for this new chapter in our family's lives.

There is a copy of De Oceaan Post, dated February 1964; this was in their room on their ship. This newspaper played a significant role in world politics and trade both during and postwar. In this edition, there is a list of cities and important information coming out of an array of metropolitan centres. Here are a few entries.

VIENNA: 28 Hungarians, Czechs and Poles, having been visitors to the Winter Olympics games in Innsbruck, did not return to their home countries, but asked for political asylum.

PARIS: police here arrested a Frenchman and 3 Tunisians suspected of organising white slave traffic of French girls to West Germany and Dakar in Senegal.

NEW YORK: President Johnson agreed to allow the American hat-making industry to promote the sale of the LBJ-model version of the five-gallon Texas hat.

My family was beginning an epic journey, travelling to America, embracing the dream of freedom and opportunity so many sought. It was a pivot point for us.

Mother wrote a lengthy letter to her sister about the trip across the Atlantic. She would tell a tale of wild weather, and how they survived, spinning a story of being terrified of being dragged down to darkness at the bottom of the ocean. An excerpt would reveal her fears.

> As we were getting over the seasickness, the fun was over—we had rough weather. I was scared. Anytime now I thought I'll meet Davy Jones. Everything was rolling from side to side and front and back. Eating at the table was a nightmare. Holding on to your food, the table and chair. The Steward would wet the tablecloth to stop everything from sliding off. One day it was so bad that the only other passenger, a Mrs Richardson (typical Brit at sea) fell in her cabin, cut her face open, sprained her wrist and was covered in blue and black

> bruises from sliding on the floor from one side of the cabin to the other before she could get her balance.

I have a limited personal memory of this trip as I was only three. Mostly it's fragments of feelings and a sense of visceral experience.

The seas were turbulent. Father and my brothers were often in their cabins, seasick. The roiling sea had no effect on me, instead, I relished in the excitement of crashing waves and salty sea air.

There is a mental image of me standing at the railing, waves crashing against the hull of the boat. This meshes into feelings of excitement. The railing is about a meter high, with three rungs. I clung valiantly to the middle rung, tiny fingers holding firm. I can even hear my boisterous laughter, confident because I was being held securely by a rope. In my mind, I see Mother standing behind me. Mother wound the rope, which she had firmly attached to my waist, several times around her wrist and hand. I feel a sense of safety, knowing Mother was holding me. I was drenched, covered in sea salt, eagerly leaning into the stiff breeze. Was this a simple, but perhaps profound, perspective on a mother's love? She sacrificed her own comfort to give her child the opportunity for new experiences? Why is this experience so tangible to me?

On the night of a big storm, my crib was not locked down. Rocking back and forth in the storm, I remember crying out. Father came to me. I raised my arms for comfort and instead was belted across the face and told to shut up as he locked down the crib. This was the moment *Annie* became. I created another person to handle the pain of something striking fear into my child's heart. *Annie*'s emergence forever altered me, forcing this body to adapt and survive.

Love at First Sight

'Hey, Joe!'

'Carry your bags, miss?'

'I get taxi, take you where you need to go?'

This was the chaos greeting us as we walked out of Ninoy Aquino International Airport. We were back in the Philippines. Everything about this place felt familiar, connected. From the clatter and rabble outside the airport terminal, the humidity and smog, and the cacophony of people; all this settled my heart. I have never understood how this existence brought my senses alive; I simply accepted it as a measure of my connection to this place.

Tom held on to our bags, I held on to Maria. She was absorbing the first sights and sounds of her birth country. I was terrified of losing her in the crowd. When we went shopping in Australia, it was hard to lose her because her dark skin stood out in a mostly white arena. But here, she blended in with all the other Filipinos. I was afraid someone would snatch her from my arms and she would disappear into the crowd, never to be found. Whatever the reason, I held on to her hand firmly as we made our way to the bank of taxis where we would pay far too much for our trip to the hotel (but still pennies on the dollar compared to Australia).

We dared to believe we were more seasoned travellers this time, staying at The Fernandina, a small, clean hotel in the heart of Quezon City in Metro Manila. Other families who had travelled recently recommended it to us. Staff were pleasant and knew enough English to help us check in. The three of us and our luggage barely fit in the elevator—a small part of the cultural experience. The best part was the food. It was a buffet breakfast, full of Filipino staples like rice, eggs and green leafy vegetables, along with fresh tomatoes and crunchy cucumber, but also *champorado* (a chocolate-styled breakfast rice), *tosilog* (cured meat) and *longganise* (sweet pork sausage). Coffee was my personal challenge. It was instant, with something called CoffeeMate to provide a certain level of milky goodness. And lots of sugar to hide the bitterness. I adjusted.

Another wonderful treat for us was Kate. She flew in from Canada to join us. Spending time with my dear friend in this place, where we shared memories, was a gift. I asked her to fulfil a specific task: to be Maria's special chaperone. Maria could easily get jealous if she wasn't the centre of attention, so having Kate along meant her days would be full of fun and adventure with *Ninang* Kate, while we were bonding with our sons. She would spend a week with us and then head up-island to visit friends in Baguio.

The next day, we waited impatiently for our ride. ICAB acknowledged our previous relationship with the orphanage and allowed the staff to come and pick us up, instead of the normal handover. Mama G had taken care of the logistics and would contact us when they arrived. To pass the time, I had Maria firmly ensconced in front of a Filipino TV show.

Filipino time is a fluid concept, so it was no surprise when, almost an hour after our scheduled meet up time, the hotel phone finally rang. Our transport had arrived and were waiting in the lobby. I looked at Tom and gave him a half-smile. 'Here we go!'

The grin on his face was all I needed. We were here. Our dream was coming true; we were about to complete our family.

Maria was already dancing around, ready to meet her new brothers and visit the place that had been her first home. I wondered how much she would remember? Other families reported their children felt scared and wary or even wondered if they were being abandoned when returning. I sensed none of this with Maria. She was bouncing around, excitedly chatting with Kate.

We crammed our stuff into the tiny elevator and made our way down to the lobby.

Seeing Mama G, her smile and gentle demeanour immediately settled my heart.

'Hello Po!' she said, warmly embracing me. 'Sorry we are late. We had errands.' Then she smiled, swiftly moving to the purpose of our trip. 'Are you ready to meet your boys?'

'Mama G! Mama G!' Maria squealed, wrapping her arms around the woman who had been such a formative part of her early life. The lobby filled with laughter. For Maria, there was no question, no wondering. The Philippines was her first home, and she rocked it.

Everything seemed to melt away—the emotional pain of this journey, the struggles with DoCS, the psych report, waiting for medical clearance. We were here. We would soon meet our boys. I could rest easy.

Full of energy, Maria monopolised the conversation as we headed east, out of Manila. She sat between Mama G, Lilly and Irene, who Maria remembered from when she lived at the home. Her effervescence was captivating. They tried simple English phrases with her, laughing and smiling. Carers rarely got to see children after they'd left the orphanage. This was a firsthand opportunity for them to see the importance of the surrogate role they played in her life.

'My teacher is the best. I'm in Year One. I'm learning maths and how to spell, but my favourite thing to do is draw.' She drew in a breath and continued. With no one to stop her, why would she? Mama G looked at me and smiled.

'I have some great friends, and I love to run around outside and play!'

Lilly was holding her hand and smiling, barely understanding a word as Maria rambled on. Somewhere in the delightful cacophony, Irene said to me in stilted English that she was beautiful. Seeing Maria thrilled them. I could only smile and say thank you. There were no words to describe how much these women meant to me.

Like our previous trip to pick up Maria, we passed out of concrete jungles and telephone wires into the hills of Rizal. Our skyline became dense palm trees and green hills. Highways became small two-lane roads as we passed through villages with mats laid out for drying rice from the nearby paddies. There were racks as tall as houses where hundreds of small milkfish hung, drying in the sun.

We stopped at a roadside *sari-sari* store, no more than a bamboo hut, but full of all the corner store treats, getting out to stretch our legs. The staff purchased icy drinks in plastic bags with straws. We drank bottled water, the only thing our stomachs could handle.

Mama G and I stood looking out over valleys carving deep lines into the landscape. I wrapped my arm around her shoulder.

'You ready, Po?' she asked with a glimmer in her eyes.

'You know I am,' I said with firm resolution.

'Two. This means you suddenly have three to care for. Your world will change a lot!' Her smile gave away the humour in understanding the depth to which our lives were changing. For Tom and me, this vision of our family, completed, was something we had prayed for. There was no need for words.

A sense of calm enveloped me as we moved further up the mountain along the Marcos Hwy. Finally, we reached the Barangay of Tanay, where the sounds of children playing and the unmistakable putt-putt of 100cc tricycles barrelling down the roadway echoed around us. There was comfort in seeing these trikes, packed to the brim with people and goods. I watched the motorcycle in front of us. A grandmother figure sat austerely in the covered sidecar with her hand draped over three large bags of rice on the seat next to her. The other hand gently gripped the metal frame. Two teenage boys straddled the back seat, another large bag ensconced in front of them. This was their mode of transport and something they had done since they were small. The trike bumped along, navigating around potholes and pedestrians. This was the Filipino way.

We passed through more villages, down meandering roads covered in a canopy of tropical fruit trees, laden with their bounty—the spiky red rambutan so heavy on some trees the branches were sinking under the weight of the fruit. More hills, twists and turns and suddenly we found ourselves back at the tall green gates I remembered so well.

Images of our first visit came flooding back; all the excitement and giddiness of meeting Maria returned. This time, our circumstances and joy were more settled, familiar, returning to a place that lived in our hearts. This time, we were coming home to our boys, Kyle and Danny. After all the doubts, frustration and angst, everything felt right. The driver beeped, and the big green gate swung open. The van pulled in and came to a stop. As soon as the side door opened, Maria bounded out, as if she had never left. She was a long-lost member of an extended family, returning to pay her respects to those who had cared for her. Maria ran around, hugging the carers and laughing. She was comfortable enough in the security we provided to explore the sights, sounds and smells filling her senses.

Tom and I stepped out of the van, quietly drinking in the joyful calamity of this place. We talked to a few of the carers who remembered us and dodged a few children running around as the busy-ness of the world seemed to fade away. The green roofs, the whitewashed besser brick buildings, the sound of children laughing—these were moments I treasured, painting mental pictures to retell later, so our boys would never forget the precious stability and love this place had been for them.

As I turned around, a small body was thrust into my arms. I instinctively reached out; it was Danny. My heart melted as he stared at me with his curious big brown eyes. Not blinking, just looking at the strange person who held him. I murmured hello and stroked his arm, feeling his reality. His tiny hands, his flat nose. My heart was full.

I glanced over to see Tom experiencing the same thing as one of the carers dropped Kyle into his wide embrace. There were no tears or tantrums, simply curiosity. I watched Tom stare in absolute wonder at his new son. We had our boys, they were no longer a heart song, they were real.

Mama G smiled and laughed, beckoning us to follow her up the stairs to the familiarity of the guest quarters. It was time to bond as a family of five.

Origins: Immigrants

Our first home in Texas was a rented duplex on Bullcreek Road; a quiet suburban area of Austin. There is a receipt for activating water and electricity for $30 dated 1964. We stayed here until the Parents purchased a house.

In these early years, Father went on numerous business trips, sending obligatory postcards showing his destination location, with a brief paragraph describing where he was and signing them, *Love to all, Dad*. He travelled across middle America and even took a trip to Canada. Mother went on outings with the International Wives' Group, which was attached to the University. Mother also became involved with Laguna Gloria, a local arts community offering work-spaces and workshops for budding artists.

We moved to our brand-new home in the hill country outside of Austin. Mother's sister and her husband were our first visitors. There is a picture of them standing with Mother and my brothers in a dirt driveway. There are more pictures circa 1965 of the house, a driveway and lawn edging gradually taking shape. The boys each had a dog; their names were Bimbo and Knight.

Suddenly, there are more pictures of me. Images which I associate with feelings and reactions from *The Girls*; I sense these are their cognitive memories. There is a picture from 1964 showing me beginning to stack on weight. In my mind I can clearly hear Mother making excuses, saying it was baby fat and I would grow out of it. Memories and photos collide. The embarrassment of the child in those photos is palpable as Mother tried to justify my rotund features. There are images of picnics in Zilker Park, brothers in Scout uniforms and Father's continued absence as he visited other atomic engineering facilities.

Mam came over to visit from England. We took her on sightseeing trips around Central Texas. It was all still new to us, and everyone had great fun as we explored San Antonio and even ventured to Laredo, on the Mexican border. Pictures of me continue to pop up. A fat, stout little thing, but with a smile on my face and a dance in my step. I stare at these images wondering which of *The Girls* this is. *Annie* confirms it is her. She lived most of our social-facing life, while the quiet dark moments were what *The Girls* lived for.

Somewhere in this new world, my life (*Annie*'s life) changed. We lived 5 minutes from Father's friend, Stanley Peters, the expat who helped him get a job at the University of Texas. Much of this part of my life is hidden from me. The only things I know are what *The Girls* choose to share. What I am sure of is this is where the underbelly of abuse started in earnest. It was Father's relationship with Stanley Peters that gave Father access to a group who enjoyed children and the perverted pleasure they could find with them. I was easy fodder.

Familiar Things

The guest cottage above the kitchen was just as I remembered it. A little worse for wear, it remained cozy and welcoming. Since we'd picked up Maria, dozens of families had come through, taking respite in these quarters as they got to know their new family member, traversing the stairs, sitting on the couch or in the rocker, their sole goal to bond with their child. Staff brought some *merienda* up for us—bottled water, rambutan and oranges, along with some packaged cookies, ensuring our tummies didn't get sick.

In the rush to get organised to travel, I had forgotten clothes for the boys. I embarrassingly admitted this to Mama G. She laughed and assured me she would handle it. She was generous as always. It was a simple oversight on my part—in the excitement of preparing to travel, I had assumed we would have time to buy a few things in Manila before coming up to the home. We took along presents for the staff (they always appreciated chocolate), and we had cash to buy more substantial gifts, like rice and canned meat, so staff could also feed their own families. We easily focused on our own needs, forgetting the home's staff also lived meagrely, and often, the children in their care ate better than their own children. This was saying thank you in a tangible and practical way for the love they had poured into our children. It was the least we could do.

Not long after, someone gently pressed a small bundle of clothes into my waiting arms. I was unconsciously rolling into my life with three children. This was just the beginning of a carousel ride defining my existence as a mother, and I relished it.

Kate understood we needed time to ourselves and went down to the room they'd prepared for her. She smiled gently at me before leaving, sharing in the joy of our family being complete.

We sat on the floor with the boys, reading and talking to them. (I remembered books, but not clothes! Go figure!) We were taking every opportunity possible to begin the gentle process of becoming a part of their lives. Such a funny thing, really. They understood nothing we said; we simply trusted our hearts would speak for us, and hearing our voices would help them become familiar with us. I pulled out a book called *The Aussie ABC's*. Both Kyle and Danny happily played with the books and touched the strange pictures of the Australian creatures I showed them. Tom was in the middle of it all, now a proud dad of boys. He reclined on the floor, and the boys leaned into him as he took his turn to read. Maria was trying her own version of bonding by insisting they sit on her lap, she was stamping herself into their lives as their big sister, saying a few simple words in Tagalog she had relearned in the few hours we'd been there. Inasmuch as we were navigating our new family, Maria was coming to terms with being *Ate*, and bonding with her brothers.

Our plan was to stay at the orphanage for one night. There were too many of us, and we knew if we stayed too long, it would disrupt the necessary schedule for the rest of the children. Selfishly, it was important for Kyle and Danny to develop their new identities with our family; the orphanage holding a treasured place in their history, but not their future.

After a surprisingly good night's sleep and a simple breakfast of rice and eggs, we wandered around the complex, saying good morning and letting the boys run and play. It was important for them to have these last moments with the other children.

Mama G came wandering through the big green gates. She lived across the street from the home on orphanage property, in a house aptly called *The Pond House* as it sat on the edge of a large pond. It was a two-bedroom brick home with a small kitchen and living area.

She asked if we would be okay taking our family and a few of the older children for a morning walk in the community. It was an opportunity for the older children to stretch their (and our) legs with a bit of activity. So, with a dozen children in tow, and the boys in our charge, we took a stroll down the lanes of this beautiful town. Kate and Maria brought up the rear, talking and nattering.

My heart was full of family and the familiarity of this amazing country. We wandered the streets, kids in uniform off to school on the back of motorbikes while roosters crowed in the background. Stopping at the nearby *sari-sari* store, we purchased drinks and lollies for everyone (and enough for the children back at the home). The orphanage was on a long, moderately trafficked road, with jeepneys and trikes passing by. It was also the start of the day, and kids were going to the state high school. As we walked by the facilities, we saw students playing basketball on the courts. This was common in the Philippines, where basketball was the unofficial national sport.

My heart settled, and not just because we had our boys. I was back in the Philippines, amidst a culture that had long dwelt in both *Annie*'s and my heart. I hoped in some way, *Annie* was finding this healing. It was also a reminder to me of being MPD. Often, I would scoff at myself for remembering this fact, but it was different today. In this moment and in this place, I was at peace with who I was, and from what I could discern, *Annie* and *The Girls* seemed content as well.

A small motorcycle slowed as it approached us. It was Bernadette, she had worked at the home when we travelled to bring Maria home. There was instant recognition on Maria's part as she ran over to hug her. Bernadette smiled at us and came over to say hi, talking for a few minutes. Then, out of the blue, she offered Maria a ride on her motorbike.

Maria jumped up and down in excitement. 'Mummy! Please! It would be so fun!'

My brow furrowed. I looked at Tom for support; he shrugged his shoulders and smiled. My protective mothering instinct kicked in. I was trying to figure out how to say no without offending Bernadette. As if she knew my mind, Mama G quickly stepped in, smiling. 'She will be fine. Bernadette will be careful.'

I breathed out quietly. 'Okay. You can go.' I smiled at Bernadette. 'Please be careful.'

'I promise, Po!' she said, helping Maria put on a helmet. Mama G and Bernadette exchanged a few words in Tagalog. I was hoping they were words of warning.

Without a second thought, Maria jumped on the back of the motorbike. I saw my precious daughter waving at me, barely looking back, with not a care in the world as the motorbike disappeared down the street.

Mama G put her arm on mine for assurance. 'She will be fine; Bernadette will take good care of her.'

I exhaled, 'I'll hold you to that!' Then we laughed and began making our way back to the orphanage, the rest of our tribe in hand.

Origins: Visceral Memories

I continued looking through the treasure trove of history I had and found a picture which brought back visceral feelings for me. I know this is *Annie*, but I cannot deny a thread of myself somewhere in this image. I wander not just through the picture, but other memories *Annie* attaches to this photo. It has no date by which I can determine my age, but I look around seven years old.

Annie is sitting in a rattan chair in the living room; a towel wrapped around her head. Mother would have just washed her hair in the kitchen sink. *Annie* has a serious look on her face and a stack of books cradled on her lap. On top is a Golden Book version of *The Jungle Book*. Reading would have been used to help occupy time while Mother tackled the inevitable mess of her thick hair.

I am drawn to the physical feel of the objects in this photo; they become quite real to me, shared moments with *Annie*. If I close my eyes, I can almost run my hand over the rattan armrest, feeling each bump and crevice. My fingers linger, rubbing back and forth, up and down, the repetitive motion soothing. In this picture, behind

Annie is an empty space with a small card table. This would become Mother's art corner, where she would paint for hours, sitting on a stool. It replaced the rattan chair, where *Annie* would have her hair brushed and combed, with varying degrees of success.

The coffee table also stands out. Again, in my mind I can run my fingers across slats, or thumb through the National Geographic magazines piled in one corner. *Annie* would often run her fingers over tactile objects as a grounding tool—something I still do today. There is a small bookshelf under the pass between the kitchen and living room. An entire set of *Encyclopedia Britanica* took pride of place. *Annie* would curl up on the floor and caress the spines of each volume, trying to decide which one she would lose herself in as it whisked her away to a magical escape in time and history.

There is a patchwork pillow on the couch. *Annie* often hugged this, grounding herself when the fears of what lay ahead overwhelmed her, tracing the delicate floral pattern to soothe herself. I feel a sense of this and of how it settled her heart.

A blue rug covered the bulk of the living room floor. It had numerous blackened cinder holes *Annie* would poke her fingers in. Crackles of timber would spit out flashes of fire, branding the carpet's delicate floral pattern, giving *Annie* another new object with which to soothe herself.

There is one last picture of *Annie* in this photo collection. She is a nubile seven-year-old, posing for the camera wearing only underwear. She has large plastic curlers in her hair, clearly feeling quite grown-up. *Annie* is unaware of her nakedness, of the tan line and how it accentuates her small but growing breasts. No self-consciousness or fear. In this moment, it was all about the curlers, mimicking Mother and craving to please and spend time with her.

Family Time

Before I knew it, we were piling into the van, leaving this time as a complete family. A few of the staff had meetings in Manila, including Mama G. We would spend a night with them at a beach-side resort in Batangas before they continued on their journey, leaving us to spend time together as a family in this idyllic location.

It was simple accommodation by any standard. We slept in *nipa* huts with fans to help keep the humidity at bay. Using the resort's basic outdoor grill, we cooked fresh food purchased on site or from the vendors who walked the beaches.

On the first night, with the orphanage staff still there, we cooked a BBQ and sang karaoke. Maria and I made everyone laugh as we belted out songs like *Dancing Queen*, and they even had a Wiggles song or two on the playlist. Danny and Kylie watched, soaking in this new way of life. Grinning, and engaging with the familiarity of the carers who were with us. We had them up far too late, but did it matter? We needed to be flexible, and the experience of being together was more important than bedtime. There would time for rules and routine once we were back in Australia.

After many hugs and smiles, the staff left the next morning, and we set about the joyful job of getting to know Kyle and Danny. Batangas would be our home for a few days, where we relaxed as a family. We played games, read stories, held hands—anything we could think of to earn their trust. Maria was fabulous, taking on the fun-loving big sister role, laughing and playing as they swung each other in hammocks and made sandcastles.

Maria and Kate spent time on beach walks, determined to collect seashells, returning with buckets full. It became a family affair to sit outside our *nipa* hut, sorting through the treasure to see what we could make—jewellery, wind chimes and even a simple checkers game. I was never so grateful for Kate as I was now; she was a friend and a rock, filling a need for us no one else could. Because she was adopted and a social worker, she intrinsically understood the children's nuanced behaviour and Maria's jealousy. She also had a history in the Philippines, having travelled over with *Annie* as a young adult. More than anyone, she got the vibe of the place and the hearts of our children.

We began to play and relax in this tropical paradise, understanding each other as a family, wandering along the beach, looking at fishing boats and weaving tales about what they did out on the water. Kyle and Danny understood little of what we said, this was about emotional bonding. They would happily go between Tom and my hands or run free but never venturing too far from our reach as we wandered down the beach. This made me smile. It meant they were already beginning to see us as their safe place.

The boys had their first beachside water encounter. Just like their sister, it was a strange new experience. Unlike with Maria, my fears about their ability to adapt to this experience quickly dissipated. We stood at the edge of the sea, dipping in toes and testing out this shimmering glassy expanse in front of us, the vastness of the South China Sea lapping at our feet. I could see in Kyle's eyes the utter exhilaration as he walked out into the gentle water, laughing as it lapped around his feet. Danny was more unsure, and he and I sat down at the water's edge. I patted the water, making little splashes, letting it run down his legs while he dug his wiggling toes into the sand. He watched in awe as Kyle, holding Tom's hand, pressed further into the surf, water splashing his knees and waist as he laughed, venturing further out. Danny and I laughed and applauded when Tom started throwing Kyle gently up into the air, cradling him on the way down, letting him splash gently into the water.

This was freedom. Kyle and Danny had been safe and loved in the orphanage, a gift many relinquished, or street children did not know. Now, they were learning there was a life outside the protected and secure walls of the orphanage. Our job was to help them experience this new freedom positively, building a foundation for their future.

Once we were back in Australia, I wondered what their little minds were thinking. I loved watching them sleep, wondering if they dreamt of the Philippines or friends from the orphanage. Was their sleep full of loss and sadness, or were they finding the change to our Western ways easy, dreaming instead of new playmates and new experiences? Occasionally, I would stand in the hallway outside their bedroom and listen as they whispered, hearing their muffled giggles and conversations. My heart smiled.

I dared to hope they were falling in love with us, the way Tom and I were already in love with them. It would take time; and time we could give. It was what DoCS had said. The older a child was when they were adopted, the longer it would take for them to really bond and view us as their safe place, their family. It would be years of playgroups, playmates, nighttime stories and cuddles. We'd had months, years even, of falling in love with the thought of Kyle and Danny, of the promise of them. We needed to be patient, be their rock. It was their turn, and we needed to be a place of steadfast love as they experienced the newness of everything around them.

Origins: Conclusions

My therapist and I spent hours discussing and theorising about the Parents, what drove them to be the people my mind held images of. We would talk about pictures, memories and possibilities. I was still searching for something logical and tangible.

They were probably alcoholics, or the acceptable phrase of the day—social drinkers. There are pictures showing Father's proclivity to drinking, always a few fingers of a stiff drink held close. There are memories *The Girls* and I hold of Mother drinking and how this affected us. Nights when she would stumble into the house after a party, Father almost carrying her. Other times, she danced around the house with a glass of wine in hand. Mother's drinking readily accounted for her angry outbursts.

The most tangible evidence for me in relation to Father is the family portrait, where no historical records mention this looming male figure. It was not far-fetched to consider that this man might have abused Father's mother or the rest of the family. Father was doting and protective of his mother as a young man. It was not far-fetched to imagine how the negative impact of being in the same house with an abusive man could have tainted Father's perspective on women. Were both Mother and I chattel to be possessed and used, something he learned from watching his own mother being treated this way?

Before looking at these photos of their history, I never imagined Father might have struggled with postwar PTSD; shell shock, as it was called then. Reflecting on the images in this historical chronicle, alongside memories of his unwillingness to discuss his life in the war, could certainly explain his behaviour. Even the risk-taking and excitement of his sexual tendencies attest to someone willing to live on the edge to numb the pain of their history.

My therapist also mentioned Mother's possible mental health struggles. Narcissism—Mother's selfish behaviour and lack of involvement in anything positive for me. The world needed to revolve around her. I don't think I would have seen this possibility if I hadn't had my own children. My inclination has always been to sacrifice, do anything, be anywhere, to ensure they knew my love and support. Mother always put her needs first. So yes, narcissism was something I had to consider.

Bipolar and Borderline Personality Disorders. I have memories of Mother having intense mood swings and sudden bursts of anger followed by a joyful verve for things she loved. She was engrossed in the life she lived with Father; her goal was sensory happiness. She lost her perspective on reality. Although less evidence supported this diagnosis, it was part of discussions with my therapist.

After the research and investigating, the only things remaining were conjecture and assumption. I could theorise or even fictionalise, but there was no hard-core evidence of my observations. However, revisiting these photos and information from an investigative perspective, with questions rather than assumptions, at least felt more honest and truthful. Questions remained; insufficient information meant no absolutes. But at least I had allowed myself to grapple with possibilities.

Birth Mother Reflections

Both times in the process of our adoption experience, we were keenly aware of the role our children's birth mothers played in their lives. We knew time would hold them in memory. Their role as the first person who loved and cared for our kids deeply was something that would never be lost. We were grateful for the meticulousness ICAB applied to investigating and providing information about families of origin.

We had names and locations, and a few pictures, holding on to these precious jewels for our kids. It was important to us that their birth mothers be remembered as a tangible part of their lives and history, whether we talked about them or not. Each of them would forever carry their birth mother's presence, held tenderly in their hearts.

Both birth mothers were young, victims of their circumstances. Their case reports gave us enough information to be acutely aware of this. Very different stories, yet the same. Stories of strength and perseverance, trying to make the best decisions they could, with one goal in mind: to make sure that their child survived and had the best life possible.

We had more information than many families who adopted from overseas. Information about birth mothers in the China program was almost nonexistent. It was the same with other countries, too. We knew how fortunate we were. When our kids were young, we used the pictures and stories from their time at the orphanage to help keep memories of their birth mothers alive. We prayed for the safety and happiness of our children's birth mothers. And we always talked about the strength of character they had. Carrying our children, giving birth and then ultimately relinquishing them to make sure they were safe. We would be eternally grateful for the sacrifices they made for Maria, Kyle and Danny.

There are myths and preconceptions about birth mothers. Worst of all was the ignorance from those who said giving a child up for adoption was the simple choice; that the birth mother should have tried to keep their child and raise them. No one knows the circumstances leading a mother to give up her child. To assume the worst made me angry.

I had fallen in love with each of my children before I met or knew who they were, and I had no biological bond. How could I think their birth mothers would not have similar feelings? And probably stronger? To love them, they made the ultimate sacrifice, ensuring they would have better lives. I'm honest enough to admit I'm not sure I could have done the same.

I am grateful that as my kids have grown, we've been able to learn more and even have some contact with their families of origin. We've learned about how they are doing and how they've taken control of their lives, having the capacity to have their own new families, which are healthy, happy and full of the typical challenges any family should have.

I would love to say that the theme of constantly keeping their birth mother's presence alive was something we did often. But children grow, and as young adults now, they are making their own way in the world. We talk only occasionally about their birth mothers now, but they are proud to be Filipino and have many Filo friends, showing a genuine interest in the culture and news of their country of origin.

One thing we did was to keep the names their birth mothers had given them. They kept their first name; we added a middle name, and then they also took their birth mother's surname, while our surname rounded out the linguistic quartet. Saying their full name was a bit of a mouthful, but outside of legal documents, they used their given first name and our surname. This was our tangible way of honouring the place their birth mothers had in their lives.

In the end, their birth mothers deserve to find happiness, love and joy. I can only hope the moments we have shared about their families of origin and their fulfilled lives are a salve to our kids' hearts.

WRESTLING THE LIGHT

Multi-faceted Motherhood

For years, I have always skirted around discussions of Mother in therapy. Steering clear of wrestling with a complicated web of love, loss and betrayal, fearful of what exploring those truths would really mean for me. When I had done all the research and come up with no clear-cut perspectives, I realised my obsessive thoughts were not about how she behaved, but *why* she behaved that way—what drove her. What enabled her to step aside from her parenting responsibilities? I was becoming fixated on Mother.

Wrestling with being multiple and its direct effect on how I perceived my relationship with Mother became an ongoing challenge. At times, going into complete denial, I could easily say she wasn't my mother; she was *Annie* and *The Girl's* mother. Psychologically speaking, it is my/our truth. I was asleep while Mother parented my system. I appreciate this logic mystifies the neurotypical mind; it is nevertheless logical to my multiple way of existing.

My relationship with Mother was vicarious; memories built through the lens of other minds with their own perspectives on mothering. And yet, the connection—the need—for me to identify this woman who raised us as *my* mother loomed in the dark crevices of my mind. I longed to honour my need for her—a mother, a nurturing soul.

The Girls feel this longing intensely. Once, they shared an image of Mother with *Middle Girl*, where Mother stood at the edge of an abusive situation. As Middle Girl cries out for help, Mother is an opaque shadow, barely visible. A mother who stood apart, fading away, choosing to protect herself rather than intervene and defend her child. Leaving *The Girls* bereft and at a loss to understand her unwillingness to help them.

Being multiple means I instinctively feel this emptiness, whether I can find the will to acknowledge it or not. These images shared by *The Girls* were not so much an actual experience, but rather a child's heartfelt cry because their mother stood by and allowed her daughter to be used. On some level, I understand these are my feelings as well, safely wrapped up and hidden away in the heart of an alter who wrestles with memories of Mother on a daily basis.

I am left with my version of loss. An emptiness, not from the abuse, but from a lack of a relationship—from not having a mother.

And what about my own children? What about this precious gift of my own journey of motherhood? Was I trying to fill the holes in my children's hearts, while I was still being my own version of the walking wounded? Could I avoid repeating this past empty motherhood on them?

There were traits I had, things I wanted for our children, which I never received from Mother. I was determined to read books to our children and share a world of magic and wonder found within their pages. Mother (and Father, too) showed little interest in the extracurricular activities I took part in. For my children, I was always at presentations, football games, assemblies and graduations—all the important moments and milestones in their lives.

But what about the traits I resented? I am someone who loves having things around to remind me of wonderful memories and experiences in my life. Mother was this way, too—she accumulated things. It's a benign trait, but still something tying me to her.

My daughter has thick, glossy hair. I would remember the agony my hair caused me as a child. From the start, brushing and braiding were an important part of my routine with my daughter. I made sure it was a positive and fun bonding time, keeping painful knots to a minimum. My boys needed the affection and nurture from a mother investing in their interests and activities, something absent from *Annie's* childhood. Was I present enough? Did I show them my love for them, not simply saying the words?

Even though I tried my best, I still felt like I wasn't good enough, an affirmation of my childhood tapes of failure. I would be lying if I didn't admit I regularly felt terrified I was going to repeat Mother's failings with my own children.

So, I hoped, I read, I prayed. I did this for these children entrusted to our care, determined they would not have the emotional failings of my life thrust upon them. As adopted children coming into a different culture, they already had enough baggage to keep them wrestling with their own identities for a lifetime. I refused to burden them with my own failings.

I wanted to be a mother, to love a child and watch them grow to be a wonderful adult. It was a simple desire at the end of the day.

Writing Their Narrative

Besides loving my children, one of my jobs as an adoptive parent continues to be building a history around who our kids' birth mothers were and honouring their unique place in our family. We also talked about the Philippines, the culture and their heritage. I found this easy, conjuring images from when *Annie* had lived there, knowing what a beautiful place it was. These things were front and centre for us when we first brought each of them home.

As younger children, the conversations were simple, safe and manageable. We would talk about the orphanage and the carers, painting a picture of security and the nurturing each of them had. They had playmates and life experiences for them to remember always. We would pray for birth mothers at the dinner table—a blessing for their happiness, peace and security.

We tried to anticipate what their questions might be through a gentle narrative about a birth mother's love and wanting the best for each of them. But inevitably, the questions would come. The first and hardest was, 'Does my birth mother love me?' Even though we hinted at their birth mother's love, it was as if in their own asking, they were taking agency. They were ready to begin their own journey of understanding their history.

Finding the words to answer this question of a birth mother's love directly was something I'd been fearful of for a long time. I scripted my response carefully. With confidence, I replied, 'Of course she does. She loved you so very much and understood she couldn't provide for you and asked Mama G and the carers at the orphanage to watch over you until we could be your family.'

Those early conversations were straightforward. A child's mind embraced our words, laying the groundwork for a beloved story—a birth mother's love, despite their absence. This was our job: to help them get through the loss.

As they grew, the questions became harder. Why did they leave me at the orphanage? Why couldn't they have tried to keep me? They were harder to answer because we wanted to be honest, but were desperate to save their young minds from the pain of their history. To ease into these questions, we began discussions about the reality of life in the Philippines: rampant poverty and homelessness. We discussed what these struggles would have meant for their birth mothers and their own daily struggle to survive. The generality of these conversations quietly settled their hearts.

In those early years, the information we shared always came back to one simple truth: the depth of love their birth mothers had for them, and the heart-wrenching decision to leave them at the orphanage, ensuring their safety and future.

The day would come when they had the right to know their entire story. The journey, everything we knew, wrapped up in the questions we asked of Mama G and the carers at the orphanage, along with the official case report.

For Maria, it was unplanned and too soon. She was barely 10, swiftly moving towards the hormonal height of puberty (the experts were spot on about Asian girls going through puberty sooner than Caucasians). I walked into the living room one day to find her sitting on the floor, surrounded by paperwork she'd pulled out of her adoption album. She was reading, as best she could, her case report. We had always told our kids they could look at these keepsakes, perhaps idealistically thinking the photos of the orphanage and early life would be all they were interested in. Instead, Maria engrossed herself in trying to read her birth family's history. They were concepts even an adult would have a hard time processing, let alone a child. And in typical Maria style, the questions came thick and fast. I answered as best I could, trying to find gentle terminology to soften the edges of the loss and pain for both Maria and her birth mother. Gratefully, she didn't fully understand the scope of what we were talking about. It was more important to lay the foundation for future conversations, where Tom and I could share the heavy burden of what those early years were.

The boys were 14 and 16. We'd already discussed a few of the difficult aspects of their heritage, but hadn't gone into detail. This time, I was simply not ready for the difficult conversation. There was no easy way to talk about it, and I had been avoiding it for far too long. Knowing I couldn't wait any longer, I asked if they wanted to read their case reports. An emphatic yes was the instant reply.

A few days later, we sat down at the dinner table and handed each of them a copy of their report.

'These are yours,' I said. I watched as they read quietly and thoughtfully about their early years, drinking the words into their souls. There were quiet tears from both of them and a few giggles from stories about life in the orphanage—their quirks, boisterousness, laughter and sibling love. These are traits I am delighted to say continue to this day.

Being typical teenage boys, they had few questions. They asked instead about the absence of their birth dad. They had photos of their birth mum, but not their birth dad. I said I could make some inquiries through channels I had in the Philippines and see what I could learn, if they wanted. Of course, was their reply. After some sleuthing, I received a photo of their birth dad, his family, and some information about their lives and shared this with the boys.

Did I expect an emotional response? Being a mother, it was what I hoped for. But they held their feelings deep in their hearts. It wasn't until a few years later that I would understand, at least for Danny, the depth of his feelings.

I asked one evening, 'If we went back to the Philippines, would you want to meet your birth dad?'

The response was direct. 'Yes, because I'd like to beat the crap out of him.'

The lot of an adoptive parent is wondering how to reveal and talk about the truth of our children's lives. Was revealing these hard truths fair? I'm not convinced this is the right question. I think it's more about our child's right to know their story.

All of us have parts of our lives that aren't pretty, things we don't want out in the open for the world to make comment on. This was certainly my life, but it didn't mean I could ignore it. I also knew we had to give our children all the information, age-appropriately. Tom and I could be there, patching up wounds, weaving a story to fill those chasms of grief, loss and abandonment. Instead, painting a narrative about strength and courage in the face of hardship, not a fragile image easily crushed. We believed the truth would make them stronger.

There will always be questions, both spoken and unspoken. My job now is to answer those questions as best I can, in truth and honesty. Sometimes they ask tricky questions without clear-cut answers. And sometimes, those questions have presented themselves differently at different ages.

Why did they leave me?

Was I not good enough?

Why didn't they try harder to keep me?

Is there something wrong with me?

We won't always get the answers right. I willingly admit this. What I believe, even in all the truth of their history, is that they can still know with certainty the sacrificial love of their birth mother and our never-ending love for them.

Kyle recently came home from an extended holiday through Southeast Asia, which included two weeks in the Philippines. I asked him what he thought of the place. His homeland. I hoped, with all the time spent talking about his history, the people and culture, it had paid off.

He smiled, 'It was really cool.'

Bookish Love

I was determined books would never be far from my children—always accessible, at child height, and never on a top shelf where they could be forgotten, collecting dust. They needed to be engaging, fun and, if possible, gently incorporate big world issues in pint-sized characters and language. I was militantly emphatic about how important it was not only for bonding, but for language and verbal skills acquisition needed to prepare them for school. Books and reading would not be lacking in their lives. We made trips to bookstores, not just to get books but to sit in reading corners and experience the smell and presence of the written word. The joy of books—escaping from reality through the written word—was something I was denied as a child. I was determined to chart a different course for my kids.

Tom and I would take turns reading to them before bedtime. Admittedly, it was easier when it was just Maria, but even with the boys, we read each night like clockwork. We shared stories of wonder and far-off lands, stories about magical places where animals could talk and mums and dads kissed and cuddled their children, about grumpy little dinosaurs and kangaroo ballerinas in pink tutus.

We also included stories of Filipino culture and folklore. The Philippines was a country full of mystical stories about demigods who lived in the hills and brought the rain, blessed rice crops and watched over villages. The National Bookstore in Manila had numerous books telling stories of children in typical lives, but with a cultural twist. What I loved the most about these books was that on the page, next to the Tagalog story, they also provided an English translation. While these books met with limited success as bedtime reading material, they were still stories of the Philippines, available to be read when they wanted.

These bedtime moments gave us a chance to be close to them naturally. *Love You Forever*, by Robert Munsch. It was a staple for me, with its illusions of a lifetime of love given and received, coming full circle. This book was as much for me as for them; reminding them of our love for them, and how Tom and I needed their love, too.

Diversity was always important in what we read. At the top of our reading pile were books about the normalisation of adoption; about being different, looking different, feeling different. In his books, Todd Parr describes how families are formed through love, not just birth, and advocates for the acceptance of differences in all families.

I wish I could say these rituals continued. At some point, their interest waned, even in chapter books. I would give them books of mythical monsters or teenage heroes to read as they got older, but they always seemed to stay unopened on their bedside tables. As the years passed, the ritual became late-night study and requisite reading for class only. They brushed their teeth and issued me a passing goodnight. Their preference became instead to spend their last 10 minutes of screen time gabbing with mates.

I've learned this is all part of growing up. Maybe when they have their own children, it will be different. Will they look back on those childhood bedtime reads and understand how bonding those moments were? I want to leave a legacy where they, too, would feel the joy of snuggling their own children while reading bedtime stories. Feeling the soft touch of their child's skin against theirs as they read, creating and treasuring moments with them.

School Revisited

When it came to my children's academic experience, I felt like I was flying blind. When they were young, it was easier. Part of my role had been to assist with language acquisition, which naturally happened as they attended preschool. We devoured books, talking about what we read to help their understanding. By the time they were in Year Five, my own fears about academia quickly overtook any false sense of security I had about my ability to tutor them. I would look at their homework, which included what I saw as complicated mathematical equations, sending them straight to Tom.

What became clear as they grew was that my kids would each be very different in how they learned and grappled with the school environment. I felt it was my job not to be a hindrance to any scholarly prowess they might have, but to see each of them as individuals. They were different in how they worked and learned. Each having so much to offer in their own way. I reminded them often how success was not based on a grade, but on working hard, doing the best they could and being proud of their effort. It was this perspective, something I wish I had been afforded me as a child, that I hoped would carry through to their adult years.

I'm not sure how successful I've been in encouraging my children to love school. None of them have proclivities towards higher learning, choosing instead trade skills and TAFE over a university degree. Which is great—we need more sparkies and builders. I enjoy hearing about Kyle's day at work, the stories he brings home about what he has learned, or how proud his boss is of what he does. I think my struggle is more a reflection of my old-fashioned and outdated notion that to get anywhere in life requires a college degree.

They were admittedly children of the COVID generation, spending a year in relative isolation, where the only genuine relationships they maintained were online, through games and any number of questionable communication apps. Their love of school evaporated. I had given in, and each of them had phones. It was a necessity of the day, which, in hindsight, I regret.

I battled often with feelings of failure in my own academic history and struggled to translate this into something positive for my children, seeking instead to find a nugget of truth in resilience, a respectful attitude and hard work. I sought to instil in them a belief that when they try (and sometimes they'll have to try very hard), they can accomplish so much. There will always be failures, but their determination as they pick themselves up will define the outcome. My children are already successful in my eyes. And each time they fail, learning to dust themselves off and try again only makes my admiration for them grow tenfold.

Farm Life

Tom's parents were ageing. We were living in the Blue Mountains, west of Sydney, and they were on the New South Wales/Queensland border, 10 hours away in the event something happened, which was an enormous concern for Tom. The kids had settled well, both in school and in their security with us. We were their safety net in this bold new Australian world. I was itching for a change. Having turned our backyard into a sustainable venture, I was keen to do it on a larger scale. It made sense for us to explore options closer to his parents. With Tom's technical prowess, it would be relatively easy for him to find a job as an IT manager up the coast.

With this as a backdrop, we moved closer to Tom's family, finding a farm in the Northern Rivers of NSW.

We lived this country life for almost six years. The goal was simple: embrace a regenerative and sustainable lifestyle to provide for our family. I was nervous about how isolated we were. We couldn't see our closest neighbour, and it took 30 minutes to get to the nearest small town. We had 100 acres to improve, applying permaculture principles to regenerate the land. A house cow gave us raw milk, and I had a go at making a variety of cheeses, from cheddar to camembert and even a few styles of blue. We raised calves for meat or sold them. At one point, we had over 60 chickens, selling eggs and using the excess to feed our family. Baking, omelettes and ice cream were often on the agenda. We had pigs, which were the bane of our existence because they were escape artists, but they were full of personality, and in the end, tasted fabulous. The animals were part of the regenerative cycle. As we moved them around the property, the chooks would poo and scratch up all the weeds, and the pigs used their gorgeous snouts to dig up soil and turn it over. This was how I built my nutrient-dense veggie patch.

Death was a necessary part of our life on the farm. We processed meat for the table (mobile butchers are great!) or put down sickly animals. Much of this would fall to me, especially the sick chicks. I would wait until everyone had left for the day and then do the deed, putting the carcass in our long-term compost. I became quite stoic, telling myself it was all part of living on the farm. Underneath these cycles of life and death, *The Girls* were reliving memories I was not aware of. Quiet images and snippets of past experiences added to my growing anxiety. These feelings were something I hadn't experienced since the adoption process, but now they were back, coursing like a torrent through my body.

My veggie patch went a long way to feeding our family, giving us potatoes, garlic, beans, courgettes, tomatoes and my favourite, asparagus, along with a variety of seasonal herbs. Attached to this was a fenced mini orchard where one of our flocks of chickens lived. We lost most of the fruit to cockatoos, mynas, and other varying gaggles of winged creatures swooping in to pilfer these delectable delights before they were ripe. Had we stayed on the farm, the next job would have been to put netting over the maturing fruit.

There were many fun moments to remember from our country life. Bonfires blazed on weekends, and after a hard day of work for the family, we enjoyed toasting sausages on sticks and roasting s'mores to finish off this fine country fare. The kids kicked the soccer ball around, creating havoc, chasing chooks and each other. Our rescue dog, Bella, happily partook in these games.

In the early years, the boys were especially passionate about all things physical and would run races and see how far they could go on the dirt track around the property, training for their next school athletics event. The kids would have friends over, chasing each other through the paddocks and laughing. When they were older, they would stay in the granny flat we had, hanging out with mates, beginning their adventure of independence. I always loved seeing the kids tromp through the grass or down near the lagoon, leaning into a sense of curiosity about their world and the surrounding wildlife.

Snake and goanna encounters were a regular part of life, where we developed a strong appreciation for Mother Nature. Once, Danny was sitting on a fallen tree, and when he stood up, a brown snake slid out from under it and off into the grass. After a mild bout of panic, we reminded them what we had always said: if you leave snakes alone, they'll leave you alone.

When their feet could reach the pedals, Tom taught each of them to drive the ride-on mower. It was easy enough for me to grab snippets of memories I remembered fondly, bringing lightness to the intangible anxiety growing in my heart.

The slow pace of the regenerative progress caught us off guard. Practically speaking, we were naïve. Tom worked in a demanding, full-time job and barely had the capacity to do farm chores on the weekends. I think because I was there every day, doing what I could, I couldn't appreciate his need for downtime on weekends, which was when I wanted to ramp things up. Tom needed to rest, the kids wanted to play, and I lived week-in and week-out with the undone things on the farm. I pushed very hard for Tom to engage, which tired him out even more and drove a wedge between us.

Isolation was an enormous factor in my mental health, even with my natural tendency towards being an introvert. Tom would leave for work, I would watch the kids dance off to the street corner where they would catch the bus, and suddenly, I was alone. Most days, there was no social interaction. I looked at emails or turned on the TV, but there would be no calls, no human voices to keep me in the present.

Some days, the loneliness would hit me like a brick, others, like a gentle wave. I became dissociative, losing hours of time each day, somehow managing to find normality before the kids came home from school. In each case, I would shake it off and get on with my constant list of daily chores, ignoring the simmering internal signal telling me something was amiss.

This aloneness was a breeding ground for doubts about my life and who I was.

I finally dared to consider something was going on with *The Girls,* but they were so far removed from my daily life I couldn't put together how their underground turmoil was affecting me. Instead, deep feelings of shame and anxiety became the norm, and I felt like I was a failure in every way possible, whether as a parent or partner. I had no one to provide me with objective feedback or perspective as I struggled to manage these overwhelming feelings. I became quietly suicidal, wishing for any sort of ending to take away the pain I was feeling.

Forced Do-Over

It was in the midst of this chaos, with emotions overwhelming me, and Tom and I growing further apart, that *Annie* returned. It was unexpected and volatile. We were in the midst of what had become another predictable argument over dwindling finances, and I stormed outside, desperate to put some distance between us. Tom followed, and a yelling match ensued.

And then, I felt her, *Annie*. Did I wake her up? Was she already lurking in the near recesses of my mind? She's never shared this with me. What I do know is I felt a shift, my head was exploding, and she was there. A presence, taking up space in my brain, claiming it as her own. Not exclusively this time. Not like when I disappeared on the boat trip to America, but instead, a shared life.

I was alone as I tried to deal with this revelation. Voices that had only been a reference because of my shared history with *Annie* were now real and tangible. *Annie*, with all her perspectives, attitudes and anger became as real to me as my physical family. I was aware of other alters, too. There was *Pretty Girl* who wanted to be beautiful for

Mother, *Little Girl*, who owned experiences of abuse, *Runaway Girl* who fought to free them from their life and *Slut Girl*, an alter created to find enjoyment in the sexual experience of abuse, finding a way to ease the pain. And there was *Angry Girl* and *Angry Woman*, alters whose purpose was to hold the pain of their lives. The lives and faces of alters seemed unending, devastatingly overwhelming.

I kept a list of the names and descriptions of these alters in a journal. A reference point to make sense of them, of *The Girls*. I had to figure out what to do next.

The apprehension and overwhelm ramped up, and the downward spiral of suicidality intensified. I needed help. I needed therapy if I was going to survive and be the mother my children deserved. Grateful for *Annie*'s memories from her young adult years, when the help of a therapist had been a positive impact on her life, I used this as my barometer, hoping it would benefit me as well. I did a bit of investigation and finally found someone who had worked with clients who had MPD before.

With the help of this new therapist, I started re-learning things about myself and my system of alters. Things I had avoided for far too long. I had to face the reality that even during the adoption process, the anxiety that loomed like a dark cloud over me constantly, was my system subtly influencing me each day. I began to make sense of why I'd had so much anxiety on the farm and identified the triggers, from processing animals to my relationship with Tom.

Part of therapy was understanding my system and their role in my life. I would mull over *The Girls*, often. Talk to them, writing out internal conversations to share in therapy. This was full of angst, and being alone did not propel me towards an objective perspective.

I spent several months on a regular check-in schedule with my therapist, a lifeline of sorts as I tried to navigate the overwhelm of getting to know my system. At times, I lived for my therapy sessions, where thoughtful, rational discussion began pulling apart the confusion in my head.

One of the big things I was coming to terms with was the volatility of Maria going through puberty; it was proving to be challenging for the entire family. We had a few holes in doors and walls, along with the inevitable screaming tantrums. This emotional onslaught caught me off guard. Objectivity might have allowed me to see her emerging struggles with her history, understanding this was how her grief manifested. Instead, all I could see was her yelling and screaming directed squarely at me. She rarely spewed any of her vitriol at Tom, and the boys only felt the effect if they were accidentally in the line of fire. I was the primary target of her rage. Not realising this was typical of an angst-driven mother/daughter relationship, I became weary and yelled at her often—no thoughtful, calm motherly love was in my heart in those difficult moments.

This set off a whole new round of triggers for me. I began searching for information about mother/daughter relationships, how to navigate them, and how to love my daughter as she was going through her own struggles.

In this hunt, I kept coming across information about how Maria's struggles could trigger my own history of abuse. Something to do with my daughter going through puberty and this being a psychological catalyst for revisiting everything I (well, *Annie*, if I'm honest) had worked through. I had long believed *Annie* had processed our past, and it was time to move on. I was wrong. *Annie* had gone through therapy and worked through issues, not me. I became overwhelmed at what this might mean for me as I read case after case of women this happened to. Realising I'd have to process my history and life from scratch demoralised me.

Initially, therapy was about my children, working through how to be in a healthier place to be a good parent. I needed to work through my stuff, revisiting memories and feelings, so I could put my history to rest. I faced this process with a sense of dread. What kept me motivated was looking at my children as they walked in the door after school and seeing their beautiful smiles and joy of life. This immense pang of love I felt for them was my drive.

Annie provided a completely new challenge. She was having a hard time watching me wrestle with my kids' attitudes, which are a natural part of a child's growth. In her mind, children should remain small and controllable. There was some logic in this. *The Girls* were, for the most part, young and manageable. *Annie* was struggling with my children's growth (by this time they were eight, ten, and 12)—growth meant developing attitudes and perspectives about their world and having opinions which differed from mine or Tom's. To *Annie*, this was confounding. She wanted me to control them with vice grips. Her diatribes about what a horrible parent I was could, at times, be deafening.

It was six tough years on the farm. The property was as derelict as my heart. Falling apart and unable to cope, we made the hard decision to put the property on the market, hoping somehow to sell it. Making as many improvements as we could, selling all of our animals, we were finally able to find a buyer for the farm. It was my hope that this move to the suburbs would be a positive step forward in our family's lives, and for my mental health. In the end, our move meant we were closer to friends and our church.

Did leaving the farm experience alleviate my anxiety and coping challenges? No, some anxieties and challenges increased, while others faded. And yes, with growing teenage children, there were additional needs to wrangle, with kids needing to go to a variety of sporting and social events. However, being closer to town and our community provided a comfort to my heart. I was no longer isolated. I had friends and a therapist, a circle of safety. And the kids were engaged in relationships both in and out of school, giving them a springboard for their young adult lives.

Charting a New Course

As I look back on my parenting journey, the things I've done right, and the things I've done wrong, I ask myself this: how did I break the cycle? It's the question I continually come back to when I consider how relatively well-adjusted my kids are.

Maya Angelou said: *There is no greater agony than bearing an untold story inside of you.*

Has it been through wrestling with the truths of my own mother/daughter relationship that these chains have been broken? Turning over tumultuous, weighty stones of memory, listening to my heart and paying attention to *The Girls* and their stories, I have brought an untold story into the light of day. I'm not even sure it's about finding an answer to the question of why Mother did what she did. It is more about no longer hiding it. By acknowledging my convoluted history, it lost its power over me.

Mother grew up in an age where women were, for the most part, relegated to the roles of mothers and wives. To nurture a family instead of pursuing a career as a means of fulfilment was the expectation.

There is nothing wrong with this choice; women (and men) choose this option today. But it is a decision, not a societal constraint. For Mother, she had no agency; her focus would have been on cooking and making babies. The only blip in her motherhood career was her brief service in the military, where she found a sense of duty and honour. She quickly gave this up for the life of a wife, mother, chief bottle washer, and whatever else was required to run the home. Did she dream this choice of domesticity would fulfil her, when instead it didn't? Did she crave more but feel trapped by the needs of three children and a husband who was on the road frequently, his own social life filled with drinking and experiences outside of family? By the time she had me, was she tired, unable to see past the drudgery of her existence? Was I a reminder of what she had lost?

With my tendency towards research, it was no surprise when I began to seek out journals and psychology books to help me understand more about my intertwined relationship with the Parents.

Epigenetics. Big word, defined by Merriam-Webster as *the study of heritable changes in gene function which do not involve changes in DNA sequence*. I interpret this to mean I carry in my genes the biological ramifications of what happened to the Parents in their own childhoods and young adult lives. Childhood experiences may have predisposed the Parents to seek each other out. I inherited trauma and am hard-wired to experience it. Makes sense.

Dr Bessel van der Kolk, in his seminal work, *The Body Keeps the Score*, talks about this very thing:

> Attachment researchers have shown that our earliest caregivers don't only feed us, dress us, and comfort

> us when we are upset; they shape the way our rapidly growing brain perceives reality. Our interactions with our caregivers convey what is safe and what is dangerous: whom we can count on and who will let us down; what we need to do to get our needs met. This information is embodied in the warp and woof of our brain circuitry and forms the template of how we think of ourselves and the world around us. (p. 154)

On the surface, it would seem the very biological nature of my relationship with Mother (and Father too) meant I too was the recipient, genetically, of their trauma. This was a surprising and satisfying revelation for me, enabling me to put much of their behaviour into context.

There are no epigenetic connections between my children and me. From time to time, I see their biological connection with their own birth mothers and cultures, but it is usually brief fragments of time. It might be their looks or similarity to their birth mothers; the way they carry themselves or show an interest in their heritage. It is the historical question of nature versus nurture.

As an adoptive parent, I believe it is the nurture I give my children that provides a framework for their development. So, while I might not genetically have passed down my history to my children, my actions, idiosyncrasies and outlook form a part of who they are. I see it in them each day. One child's propensity to quiet contemplation, like Tom, another prone to verbal diarrhoea—one of my particular traits. These are innocuous attributes they have picked up simply because they are a part of our family.

I continued reading van der Kolk's book, and his discussion of what our children can teach us surprised me.

> ... our babies often teach us how to love. Adults who were abused or neglected as children can still learn the beauty of intimacy and mutual trust or have a deep spiritual experience that opens them to a larger universe. (p. 154)

He talks further in the same section about learning from our traumatic past through the eyes of our children, recognising our own irrational thoughts and behaviours as a promising first step toward healing. He goes so far as to suggest the very act of loving can lead to exponential change.

Throughout *Annie*'s young adult life (which is my life by inheritance), vicarious love surrounded her once she removed herself from the trauma of her family. In some ways, friends showed this love through confrontation, challenging her behaviour to help her see the possibility of change and a better version of herself. Did this honest love help *Annie* heal, and now makes me a better parent?

This is something I see in my life every day. I continue to seek help through honest friends and a committed therapist. These are all small things which remind me I am not tied to the life Mother experienced. I see my children not as pawns or pieces to be used as I was, but as precious lives to love and nurture.

The converse would have been true for Mother. Growing up in an era where the expectations of what a woman could or should do put her in a box. Did this impact her ability to see herself as someone of worth and, therefore, affect her ability to love and nurture me? Did this make her susceptible to someone like Father, drawn to him because of her own genetic predispositions? I don't know the answer to this question. Still, there is something about allowing myself to contemplate the truth of Mother's life that could have been, which gives me the strength to face the truth of my own life, and more importantly, my relationship with my own children.

Mother and I grew up in two different cycles. For her, it was a closed loop, with societal and relationship expectations trapping her. Becoming part of this cycle was her only means of survival. *Annie*, as a young adult, pried loose from the physical ramifications of an abusive childhood and used caring, nurturing, positive influences to help us see beyond our entrapment.

These days, my young adult children continue to teach me to live beyond those cycles. Their unconditional and somewhat chaotic love strengthens me. I see the difference between what I had and the possibilities of their own lives—lives I have poured into with my love. Seeing their growth and inquisitive demeanour makes my heart sing.

I must be honest; wrestling with my relationship with Mother rattles me. Acknowledging this feels like a declaration, like a betrayal of what should have been a sacred bond. I still have a propensity to blame myself. However, in the end, it was Mother, her history, her choices. I can finally see this and understand she wasn't evil—she simply had no hope. She gave up and gave in to the life dictated to her by the era, the war, and her history.

I have hope; Mother did not. Hope makes all the difference.

Football Season

'Mum, can I watch State of Origin tonight?' Kyle asked as he put his backpack on, ready to head out the door to catch the bus. I smiled. Oh, how he loved his football!

I eyed him thoughtfully. 'Well, I reckon I'll need a pretty serious payment!' His eyes went wide in terror, his brain churning over what payment I might extract so he could stay up late and watch the game. I pointed a finger at my cheek. 'I will need a kiss.'

Relief and immediate consent. His kiss, captured and treasured in my heart. Bliss!

My joy that night stemmed from sitting next to Kyle on the couch, just the two of us. My 11-year-old son normally wanted nothing to do with me, but now we were shoulder to shoulder, ready to watch this anticipated match. Popcorn and chips—tick. I told him we had to make it interesting; I would barrack for the underdog team. He rolled his eyes, smirking with a stereotypical male certainty that his team would crush mine. My heart jumped for joy at sharing these precious moments with him.

Kyle spent the evening explaining the subtleties of a game that eluded me. American football, with all its padding and clock-stopping was my point of reference. I didn't mind; it meant he talked to me. For this Australian version of football, I watched men in tight pants running with the ball and gang-tackling each other. When I got excited and yelled over a good play, Kyle would tell me to quiet down telling me it wasn't as good a play as I thought. I taught him about gridiron strategy; he taught me about rucks and scrums. He told me about his favourite players, and I said I had no idea. In the end, my underdog team won, and I was boisterously excited.

'Oh, Mum, you are so annoying!' he declared, jumping over the back of the couch, stomping off to bed with a huff.

As I snuggled under my covers that night, a contented and joyful mother, I couldn't help but wonder about *Annie.* She never had these intimate moments of bonding with Mother. I was sad, knowing this was never her experience. But also grateful at the privilege of sharing these moments with my son.

That Hair!

Maria's allocation photo triggered me the moment I saw it. Her long, dark locks transported me back to memories of yanking combs and angry words from Mother when she brushed my hair. I vacillated between being terrified of how I would respond (correction—how *The Girls* would respond) to any issues arising from managing my daughter's glorious locks and the intimate joy I hoped would deepen our mother/daughter relationship.

I saw images in my head of a terrified alter trying not to cry as Mother brushed knots out of her hair, sitting on a stool with no escape, each yank of the brush causing pain. Coming to terms with a daughter who had long, thick, luscious hair, I became doggedly determined I would not repeat with my daughter what had happened to me.

Before we travelled to pick Maria up, I went to department stores, heading directly to the beauty section, looking at all the hair clips and bobbles, collecting a plethora of bright and funky hair ties to keep Maria's hair in some semblance of control.

It became a daily routine for Maria to find her hairbrush and a few of her favourite hair ties and pull out a kitchen stool where I would wrangle her bed-head locks into a ponytail, pig tails, braids, or what quickly became her favourite, French braids.

There was the occasional accidental hard tug on her head, met with the requisite 'Mum! That hurts!' or when she was younger, simply grabbing her head and yelling out. But these were never brutal encounters; they were simply part of managing her hair. And she certainly never shied away from telling me when I'd pulled too hard.

Camping with friends in our adoption circles was a regular part of our lives. Getting Maria to hold still for a hairbrush before going out to rummage through the bush or doing somersaults on a jumping pillow was next to impossible. Instead, before we left on our adventures, I would sit her on a stool in front of a TV show, putting as many mini braids in her hair as I could. It was not uncommon for me to put her hair into over 40 tight, carefully plaited and secured braids. Her hair would stay this way for the entire trip. One or two would invariably come loose, but I would fix them with the trusty stash of hair ties I brought along. It meant coming home was relatively trouble-free, releasing her locks with inconsequential damage to both her hair and our relationship.

I admit with some sadness—and yet an undertow of pride—that by the time she reached Year Six, she took care of her own hair. She would head out for the school bus with a beautiful, bouncy ponytail bobbing along behind her. The only time my touch was required was for school pictures or some special activity.

Maria is a young adult now. She's moved away from home and is enjoying her best life. She comes home every few weeks for dinner and an evening natter (with numerous phone calls and text messages in between). Not long ago, we pulled out a movie to watch. We were happily reclining on the couch, mildly entertained by the show.

She smiled at me, 'Mum, would you play with my hair?'

'Of course, sweetie, run and get the brush from my bathroom.'

She sauntered off, returning with said brush, grabbing a few cushions from the couch and wedging herself between my legs.

My heart was light as I brushed her gorgeous hair, no knots in sight. I smiled to myself; grateful she had learned to take care of her thick mop. I braided and played with it, brushing it all to one side and then the other, relishing the feel of her silky strands as they glided through my fingers.

'You have grey hairs!' I exclaimed as I examined the translucent strand in my fingers.

'Do I! Can you pull them out and save them for me?'

I pulled out the scant few I found, obvious against her dark hair. She laughed and took pictures of the silver threads I handed her.

'You can keep brushing my hair if you like.'

I happily obliged, gently pulling the brush through, mesmerised and happy with each stroke. It was smooth under my touch, and the warmth and joy of these quiet bonding moments brought healing to the images of my past, reminding me I had done something right.

Genetics

Genetics. It's the thing binding us to our biological family. No denial is possible. Someone says, 'Hey, you really look like ...'

Your father.

Your mother.

Your grandparent.

It's biology, linking me forever to my family. I have looked at pictures of my brothers, both when they were young and as they have become mature men. My eldest brother bears an acute resemblance to Father, becoming a willowier and leaner version of his namesake. He does not carry the gut of an alcoholic. He has the same dark features, striking cheekbones and smouldering dark eyes. My other brother has captured features from both the Parents. He has the chiselled intensity of Father's face, including a long nose, but also has the roundness more akin to how Mother looked in my memories of her. His eyes have always been bright and warm.

I stare in the mirror and wonder who I look more like, Mother or Father. My mind quickly conjures a simple response: I don't want to know. And yet, while I can clearly see features of each of them in images of my brothers, I struggle to see them in me, even as they stare me in the face.

My similarities lean more toward the external features of Mother—the heavy-set rectangular body. She went deaf in one ear at some point. I wonder if this, too, is happening to me (helped along by my children, who often accuse me of being deaf).

And moles. I have dark-brown amoebic splotches on my face. There are memories of her having had surgery to remove these grotesque features. Mine are the same. One is even large enough now that my glasses will often rest on it. I should get rid of them, but I don't want to do what she did. I want my own journey. Would the craters left behind become a negative space tangible reminder of her? I can't consider this, and so I put the issue aside. It becomes too hard for my soul to bear.

My similarity to Father revolves around deteriorating health. I have asthma; it grows worse as the years pass, but I manage as best I can. Father eventually died from his asthma and the associated complications of lung failure. Is this also my destiny? I choose to believe medical care has developed enough to ensure this is not my fate.

When doing my daily puffs so I can breathe with relative freedom, I stand in front of the mirror, wondering if he took care of himself. Did he, like I do from time to time, try to believe he could get by without the daily dose of magic dust to open up his airways, ensuring his breathing wasn't laboured?

Either way, I stare at myself with my spacer and inhaler in hand, puffing in and out. My thoughts always, always linger on this disease, a quiet binder to him. And too, *The Girls* can be heard loud and clear. This thing I do makes me a living reminder of him and the role he played in their lives. It brings back echoes of his wheezing and coughing as he made his way to their room each night, keeping them on edge, terrified of what the darkness held.

My children have visual similarities to their birth families. Maria and her birth mother could easily be mistaken for sisters. If you look at pictures of Maria's birth mother when she was younger, you could blink and think they were the same person. What a precious treasure to have! Or is it a curse, a daily reminder of the woman who gave birth to her?

My sons, too, have similarities to their birth family. Danny's is more obvious. He bears a flat nose and a broad forehead from his birth mother. Kyle's similarity is assumed. He bears no striking resemblance to his birth mother, which leads me to assume he looks like his birth father. Do these things enter their minds as they stare in the mirror or look at photos?

Are they proud of this connection to their birth families? Or is it a reminder of a life they would rather forget? Maria seems to be the only one who freely acknowledges this genetic connection with her birth mother. The boys do not say. But this may be because they don't really ponder it, rather than simply not wanting to discuss the subject.

The genetics of it all, whether or not wanted, bind me to my family, and my children to their birth origins. Ties that bind. Both my children and I hold forms of trauma in our genes. And yet, why is it I crave for my children to be proud of their genetic connection to their birth families, but despise mine?

The Root of Anger

With the help of therapy, I was coming to terms with my system—who *The Girls* were, how they related to each other, and to me. This wasn't always a straightforward relationship. Often, alters created to protect my body during our childhood caused problems for my day-to-day functioning. Their need to protect me could become obtrusive and belligerent.

In this house in my head, the construct where *The Girls* live, everything is fairly well-ordered. *Annie* oversees daily routines with a sense of purpose, ensuring *The Girls* are compliant and the system functions in an orderly way. She is the enforcer of rules, enabling the system to survive. And in this house, with these *Girls*, one important rule reigns above all: no anger and no getting out of line or causing problems. Maintaining peace at all costs.

Two alters, an older and younger version of each other, have been banned from the house. They posed a threat to the peace. As a result, they sit on the edge of the sandpit in the front garden, huddled together, come rain or shine, as if their collective energy keeps them strong. My alters exist sometimes to hold specific experiences. But for these two, they hold a single emotion. Anger. This is why *Annie* and *The Girls* ejected them. Their very presence disrupts the peaceful and orderly functioning of the house. For this story, they are aptly called *Angry Girl* and *Angry Woman*.

Angry Girl existed to meet the need of holding this thing called anger at arm's length. Collectively, *The Girls* could not be angry; it would lead to physical pain. With all the injustice, from the physical abuse from Father and his friends to the emotional and physical abuse from Mother, it was up to *Angry Girl* to hold it tight, to protect the others. *Angry Girl* knew the difference between right and wrong—the unfairness of their lives—and it made her seethe. Holding these feelings because the others could not, was her job.

The Girls felt relief when piling these emotions at *Angry Girl*'s feet. It gave them a quiet strength to acquiesce to their circumstances and survive, giving this emotion away. *Angry Girl* remained stoic and resolute. Aware of the importance of her job, even as *The Girls* rejected her because they feared the danger her anger held.

Angry Girl especially hated Mother. She craved her love, and when Mother betrayed her, it made her an easy target for her anger. Mother had given over her child to be used by others for their own sinister purposes. Each of *The Girls* had their own stories, their own betrayals, and as *Angry Girl* felt their pain, it profoundly affected how she viewed everything she came into contact with. She remained quiet, knowing it was her job in the system.

And while this was her assigned role, this did not make it easy. Sometimes, anger would overwhelm her small body and rear its ugly head in the real world.

Angry Girl would secretly eat things Mother said were illegal—sweets, lollies and things for special events. She knew Mother craved a beautiful daughter and was determined she would not be what Mother wanted, because she hated her. Mother would make things for parties and store them in the outside freezer. *Angry Girl* would eat them while Mother was away. She would secretly eat as much chocolate as she could find, or anything she believed would help her be fat. It would upset Mother, and this made *Angry Girl* happy.

Angry Girl ran away from home, determined she would never be around the Parents again. They laughed as she left, only fuelling her determination. She stormed down the road and into the bush, hiding away for hours. There, in the quiet stillness, she allowed herself to dream about how her world could be different; how if she weren't angry, the Parents would love her. She hoped. She wondered. And in the end, she returned home quaking, determined to be obedient, hoping they would love her.

Like a happy ending gone wrong, she quietly entered through the back door. Father was in his chair, Mother painting in her corner. They looked at her, confident in the power they held over her.

The only words uttered as she walked to her bedroom were from Mother. 'I knew you'd be back.'

Anger, unless resolved, remains deeply embedded in the heart. It is a dormant volcano, unnoticed to the outside world. So, as *Annie* grew, anger remained. *Angry Girl* became *Angry Woman*. Feelings of hatred and venom owned her heart, fuelled by a sense of injustice about what happened to them, unresolved circumstances from their turbulent childhood cradled close. With the clarity coming from adulthood and freedom, and hidden behind the shield of *Annie*, *Angry Woman* engaged in the external world. The tectonic plates of blatant global social injustice against children and the poor caused decades of deeply held anger to pour out.

At times, it would be a quiet lava flow destroying *Annie*'s friendships or creating problems at work. In other moments, it was a giant geyser of ranting anger spewing out at the unfairness of the world, threatening her desire to live. Her only solace came from knowing her job. Embracing the dark feelings of injustice, betrayal and abandonment, she protected the others.

In this way, *Angry Woman* and *Angry Girl* relished their outcast life at the sandpit in the yard. With no care or thought for the others, *Angry Woman* and her charge thrived in the intensity of these emotions, shards of venom oozing across the ground as they relished in their hatred of Mother.

Inquisition

It was impossible for me to come to terms with the complexities of my motherhood story without acknowledging a strong and imposing figure at the heart of my wrestling: *Angry Woman*. For me, understanding her and the place she holds in my kaleidoscope MPD system is something I can't get away from. I can see the place she holds in my life, affected by a demand for social justice, whether the abuse from Father or the way I felt unjustly treated in our adoption process. These types of things showed me the influence she had, even when I refused to acknowledge it. The why of *Angry Woman*'s existence had become as important to me as understanding who Mother was.

Not long ago, quietly and in stealth, *Angry Woman* left her exiled post in the sandpit and entered the house, my internal construct for where my system of alters lives. Abandoning *Angry Girl*, *Angry Woman* covertly made her way into the kitchen. The kitchen is a place in the house representing a sanctuary from the chaotic noise of this internal home. The pristine white walls, floors and cupboards, and a white toaster, a lone item on an otherwise immaculate bench top, speak calm. This is a place where only settled hearts, those who are at peace, feel comfortable. It is not about whether they (or I) have issues and concerns resolved; it is about a sense of calm. There is no requirement to be happy, but any of *The Girls* who enter should feel comfortable enough to be exposed.

As a result, none of *The Girls* enter this space. I will not enter the kitchen. When I engage internally with my system, my eyes inevitably see the kitchen, and the restful peace it represents, but I never dare to enter. I know I am not settled; I am not at peace, and my presence would cause chaos.

Now, *Angry Woman* fills the kitchen with her presence, opening cupboards and smashing plates. Deliberately creating her own sense of chaos. I acknowledge and accept the esoteric nature of this mental foray into the house. Her presence in the kitchen contradicts the inherent rules keeping this place safe. Why has she entered the house's only safe place, intent on destruction?

My therapist asks from time to time if I have engaged with *Angry Woman* and how this might relate to my relationship with Mother. *Angry Woman*'s physical presence has become consuming.

'Have you tried to understand what's going on?' This is my therapist's regular, patient query.

'Yeah, but I get nowhere. She's pissed off I'm trying to understand more about Mother. She's breaking things in the kitchen.'

There is so much more, but I skim over the surface. I cannot bring myself to talk about it. What if voicing my fears destroys me? What fears? I wasn't sure. *Angry Woman*'s presence scared me; that was enough.

In true therapist style, he planted seeds, subconsciously encouraging me to explore the why behind my fears. His seemingly innocuous comments drew me like a moth to a flame. I felt compelled to understand, stifled in my pursuit of what drove Mother until I wrestled with *Angry Woman*. So, I retreat into my head, standing in the hallway of our house, watching her in the kitchen, invading this sanctuary, the one place where *The Girls* could feel protected.

Here in the hallway, I watch a movie reel, historical postcard glimpses of the life *Angry Woman* and *Angry Girl* lived. Trapped. Burdened with a job ensuring rejection, even by their own tribe. A reminder of why *The Girls* have shunned them, standing in judgement as they were ejected from the house and sent to the sandpit. This would be their new home, huddled together, hearts becoming darker each day with the pain they held.

I lingered like a wallflower in the hallway, watching the mess in the kitchen with a new understanding and appreciation of the enormity of *Angry Woman*'s job. Taking me by surprise, she looks at me, acknowledging my presence.

Before I can quietly slip away, she asks, 'Why the hell do you have to do this?' Instinctively, I understand she is referring to my driving need to explore the roots of our relationship with Mother.

'I'm trying to understand our history. And, if I'm honest, I want to understand you.'

She glares as she throws another plate onto the floor. I notice, for the first time, *Fairy Princess*. She is sitting on the counter, dressed in a child's nightie with rainbow wings and sparkly slippers. She holds a delicate wand in her hand, and with a gentle swoosh, the plate evaporates in a magical mist, replenishing the never-to-be-empty cupboard. *Fairy Princess* giggles. I can't tell if this replenishing of the dishes is appreciated by *Angry Woman* or not, but the partnership continues.

Angry Woman looks at me. 'Bullshit. You're only doing it because your shrink says you should. You don't really want to understand.' A pause and then an indictment. 'You couldn't understand.'

'Do you want me to understand?'

She ignores my question, instead flinging another accusation. 'Why her? Why Mother?'

I cringe as she throws a plate, watching ceramic shards splinter against the floor. 'I dunno. Mother seems to be a big blank part of the puzzle.'

'You want to forgive her.'

'I never said that.'

'Yes, you did! And yes, you do! I've heard you say to others you'd like to forgive her.'

I feel cornered, shrugging my shoulders in compliance. 'Maybe. I'd like to try to forgive her, maybe understand her better. I guess I'm hoping an exploration of her history will help me come to terms with who she was and why she treated us the way she did.'

And then a pause, because I need her to hear this: 'But I'm not there yet.'

Another plate hits the ground. Suddenly, *Angry Woman* sits down, physically spent, breathing hard. Head in her hands, she mutters, 'Why do you have to write these things? You will destroy me if you write this.'

'Like I said, I want to understand.' I am trying to be empathetic, but this is a concept I cannot imagine she would understand.

She looks at me, her eyes empty, mournful and tinged with grief. 'But she betrayed us.'

'I know.' These are the only meagre words I can find in the face of such rampant pain. Any other response would simply be platitudes.

As if shaken out of her grief, she glares, giving me her ultimate declaration, 'You're an idiot.'

Angry Woman returns to her methodical way of dealing with life. From the safety and confinement of the house, she stands up and goes back to smashing plates; this is her cathartic release. Having never been able to give voice to her anger, this physical action is her outlet. I wonder if, with every smashed plate, she is imagining all the ways she could have saved us from Mother. Retribution.

Watching her leaves me confused and empty. I have no words; it's too much for me to wrestle with; I walk away, leaving the chaos of this internal world for the reality of my day-to-day life. I'm craving the normality of family and friends.

Maybe *Angry Woman* is right. Maybe I want to forgive. But more importantly, I want to understand. What if I could piece together a story about Mother's life? Would it make sense of what she did? Would it really settle my heart? To *Angry Woman*, this would be the worst of all—to wrestle with, come to an understanding of, a woman who should have protected us. Instead, *Angry Woman* saw Mother as the one who made us a living sacrifice for one simple purpose—to make her husband happy. How can anyone forgive or understand such an action?

I suspect at some point I will have to face the truth of *Angry Woman*. She is part of my system, giving me the strength to change a generational pattern of abuse. Her awareness and, frankly, her ability to call out our history rather than try to hide it, have demanded I confront the reality of who Mother was to me, ensuring I don't repeat this pattern with my own children.

She and I battle constantly. I want to understand facts. Who was Mother? *Angry Woman* feels any exploration of this is a betrayal of my system. Is this a juxtaposition between anger and forgiveness? By trying to understand, am I forgiving, or am I letting go? Her hate has kept the system strong, balanced. And then I wonder, does she actually hate Mother, or is this all a cover-up for trying to hide the pain of everything we suffered?

Responsible Anger

When I realised my dream of seeing *SPLIT* published was, in fact, going to be a reality, I knew my kids needed to know about my life as someone living with MPD. I had told them some generalities about my abusive upbringing but omitted the multiplicity. I didn't want my children to be blindsided by unintentional or confronting comments from social media. They were young adults now, and while it might be difficult, I was sure they could handle it.

In the end, they were fabulous. They understood who I was as their mother, so this revelation regarding a part of who I was made no difference. They had questions, of course, which was good. It meant they wanted to understand. There was a sense of clarity in our relationship as they would ask about different situations and I would, rather sheepishly, confirm, *yep, I had been under the influence of an alter*. Eventually, the normalising process began, and they got who I was.

I was sick—with the flu, the lurgy—typical winter hacks and coughs where I was completely run down. I couldn't make meals or do laundry, which wasn't a big deal, except as a mother, I had this inbuilt guilt where even if I was on my deathbed, I should somehow get the basic domestic jobs done. And on top of all the day-to-day responsibilities I heaped on myself, there was an important event looming a few days away, and I really needed to be healthy. In regional Australia, it can take weeks to get in to see a GP, so I opted to go to the only critical care clinic in the area. Danny, my youngest, was also sick, so we made a morning of it.

It was a few years post-COVID, but precautions were still everywhere. There were signs telling you to wear a mask if you were ill and expansive Perspex screens keeping the sick away from front reception staff. In these situations, my anxiety always got the better of me. I could feel it rising in my stomach, a fear and humiliation I could not control. I had long since come to terms with not being able to wear a mask; putting something over my mouth was a trigger. As an abuse survivor, the sensation of the mask brought back horrific body and sensory memories often beyond my control. During COVID, I wore a lanyard stating I was exempt from wearing a mask. I no longer wore this but still carried my letter of exemption in my wallet as a quiet shield against the negative onslaught I expected. The new normal in medical facilities was for clients to wear masks if they were the slightest bit ill, and for staff to be protected by expansive screens. It made sense. These were logical precautions.

I am compliant by nature, and the sign over the intake desk said to advise reception if you had any coughing, sneezing or feverish symptoms. I should have lied.

'You'll need to put on a mask,' was the nonchalant response. She didn't even look at me as she took my details.

'I have an exemption,' I replied, shaking as I pulled the well-worn letter out of my wallet.

'Doesn't matter. We have to think about others at the clinic. If you don't wear a mask, we won't see you.' Direct and to the point.

I turned the situation over in my head; there were other people sitting outside in chairs, waiting to be seen. Why was I not offered this as a solution? Anger started to rise at the perceived injustice of the situation. Why were other attendees more important than me? Why were they allowed to wait outside, but I was being turned away? I was roiling. The anger welled up, swelling in my gut and forcing itself out. Before I could stop, I was blasting my spray of infectious droplets across every spot on the reception counter.

Horror crept across the reception staff's faces.

Th cognitive dissonance in my heart was deafening. Instantly, anger mixed with a boatload of shame. I should have controlled myself. But anger was the beast inhabiting my body. *Angry Woman*. She thrived in these circumstances, justifying her volatile outbursts.

Stepping from behind the protective screen, the supervisor immediately asked me to follow her outside to continue our discussion in, as she said, a more civilised manner.

What ensued, as my heart calmed down, was a thoughtful conversation about the professional hygiene needs of the clinic and its requirement to manage this. I even felt heard by this supervisor after I explained how masks were a trigger for my historical abuse. She even said COVID must have been difficult for me. I felt my heart settle.

I smiled weakly with gratitude. The bomb of anger was successfully defused. Someone brought chairs outside, and they welcomed

Danny and me to wait for a doctor. In the meantime, a triage nurse saw me as I waited quietly in the sunshine.

In between this, Danny and I talked about what he'd witnessed.

'Do you know what happened then?' I asked sheepishly, still nervous about what to say so as not to terrify my kids, lest they think I was psychotic.

'An alter?'

'Yep,' I sighed. 'Need to talk about it?'

'Nope. The staff were pretty shitty and rude.'

I smiled. Oh, how I loved my kids! Even as ratbag teenagers, they still showed me their love and support.

As we drove home from the clinic, I reflected on my behaviour. My immediate reaction was shame and disgust at allowing this to happen. I wanted to believe I could control my circumstances, relegate *The Girl*'s feelings and struggles to the therapist couch. I gave them no other outlet. *Angry Woman* needed a release from what she perceived as abuse by the medical staff. For her, this blowup released a pressure valve, allowing her to reset her heart and remind me I was powerless to control her.

Her outburst blindsided me. I sensed her satisfaction from the double blow of upsetting the clinic staff and causing me shame. It was retribution and a reminder; at any moment she could take charge.

A few weeks later, I received a letter from the clinic advising me I was no longer welcome to attend their facility. Apparently at 63, with staff tucked behind Perspex screens, I was a threat to their safety. I had to laugh at the lunacy of their accusation. The reality set in. I became numb, followed by shock, and then overwhelming indignity and shame. *Angry Woman*'s satisfaction at my humiliation and her hatred of the world solidified.

I was torn. It was obvious these were medical staff who did not have the training needed to identify who was or wasn't a legitimate threat. I felt cast aside, all because I was misunderstood. This played directly into *Angry Woman*'s hands, reminding me mistrust was the first and best option. The lack of training and education for front-line staff in dealing with unique and difficult situations was, and remains, a huge issue needing to be addressed. But I did not have the willpower, gumption, courage, whatever you want to call it, to challenge these false assumptions and their naïve ignorance.

I did the best I could. I wrote the clinic director a letter outlining exactly what I knew had happened. I even went so far as to include a chapter from my book *SPLIT* talking about the challenges of my diagnosis and how my inability to wear a mask was a trigger. But it did not mean I was a threat.

I had to leave it. I had done my small part to educate, and could only hope somehow it would sink in. I spoke to several medical professionals about this matter and found across-the-board agreement as to the abhorrent way that I had been treated. I was grateful at least, that in my small circle of relationships I could be satisfied in their willingness to cast aside stereotypes and stigmas.

On a personal level, I needed to appreciate who *Angry Woman* was, how in her own way, she was defending me, defending *us*. She was standing up for our rights when I simply couldn't; keeping us safe in the only way she knew how. I didn't necessarily understand or appreciate the way she protected us, but she was fighting back in the way she knew, from the history she had lived.

Wrestling Forgiveness

I naturally tend towards forgiveness. Intuitively, I want to believe the best of any person or situation. Blindly, I hope somehow good will out and right will win. I've always been this way. Perhaps it's naïve to believe people are intrinsically good, but I do, despite the ugliness in world, despite what happened to me as a child. It feels like the right thing to do. Forgiveness aids in healing relationships and letting go of inconsequential things in life. Forgive, move on.

There is also a good chance it's part of my conditioning as a child. *The Girls* wanted the Parents' love, so we always forgave whatever happened. Somehow, believing it might be the thing to end the trauma and give us a family where love abounded. It was wrong, of course, but a child wants their pony, and my system's pony was to be loved by the Parents.

Repeatedly, I am asked if I wish my parents had faced judgement for their actions. Would a court finding them guilty satisfy a need in my soul? Would this ultimate form of justice bring peace to my heart? It's a complicated question. The drive behind the word judgement is vengeance and retribution. Anger, not peace. This made complete sense. Anger, for me, doesn't let go. It holds the pain close and creates a drive in my belly, giving me a short fuse and sleepless nights. It drives *Angry Woman*'s perspective and behaviour. Sometimes, it destroys relationships. I'm not convinced the Parents receiving judgement would help me sleep any better.

Why is the drive to forgive so strong in me? I could say it stems from my faith; it is the Christian thing to do. And yes, it is, but there is also a place and, frankly, a need, for consequences. It's biblical and an important part of life and growth. If my child does something silly, I can forgive them, but for them to learn and change, there must be consequences. I knew without a doubt my desire to forgive was not about letting my parents off the hook for their behaviour. This desire to forgive was bigger than retribution; it was about freedom. More specifically, my freedom.

Did my parents deserve forgiveness? Or is justice the better perspective? After all the research, staring at pictures and putting together a sketchy and piecemeal image of the Parents' history, I could, with significant trepidation, understand why they were who they were (with the important distinction: forgiveness did not mean acceptance). From a childhood devoid of positive male influence for Mother and her dive into drinking and a self-obsessed, perhaps narcissistic lifestyle, to Father having his own issues with a questionable father figure, drinking and postwar PTSD—I could say there were plausible reasons why they were who they were. This was my driving thought: to understand who they were.

But did this equate to forgiveness? I did some brief research into the etymology of the word 'forgive', discovering forgiveness is an active word. It is done by someone. It is about the giver, not the receiver. I thought this was an interesting perspective. It was, then, a choice. Power. In my heart, forgiveness was not so much about righting a wrong with the Parents—an impossible task—it was about *my* journey, *my* healing. What I chose to do.

There is no absolution for what they did. I (and *The Girls*) will live the rest of our lives with the ramifications of their actions. But could I be the bigger person? Could I let go of them and be free? It seems an impossible, even idealistic task, but certainly something I want to strive towards. Especially if it could give me peace. In the end, this was my goal. Peace from the pain of triggers and memories haunting my system. I want to run towards this.

And then I stop in my tracks. I am terrified of what this could mean. If I'm honest, I would rather hang on to the anger. It's mine; it's *Angry Woman*'s. A tight knot in the pit of my stomach kind of anger, sustaining and empowering us in difficult circumstances. The backbone and willpower which, if I'm honest, on some days gives me the strength to get out of bed, when I would rather hide and ignore the world.

But I'm not there yet. I would be lying to say anything else. I still cower in fear of the possibility of letting go of something so intrinsic to my existence. The question demanding an answer then is: if I let go of the pain I've held so close, what do I have left? What would I fill this void with? I'm not sure at this point. I am so used to embracing the pain and familiarity of what I know, I can't imagine the alternative and what it might look like. It's as if forgiveness and moving on is right for everyone, but me.

It is the conundrum of living with my system of alters. My internal dysfunctional family. They are the parts of me directly affected by Mother's treatment. Faced with their immense pain, longing and loss, they rail (literally) against any type of forgiveness. To them, forgiveness is not healing. For them, even considering letting go of my childhood with the Parents is, in some ways, acquiescence. Worse still, betrayal. Instead, especially for *Angry Woman* and *Angry Girl*, they would rather use anger to fuel their existence. This strength lets them express what they couldn't express as children and, I daresay, gave them the ability to survive their childhood.

This is my journey and belongs to no one else. I have discussed this with my therapist from time to time, and I understand forgiveness, or as I choose to say, letting go, is my healing journey. It is not a hard and fast rule for growth and change to foist on others; it is simply where my heart is leaning.

What is more terrifying than letting go of who Mother and Father were, is coming to terms with my own instinctual behaviour around what happened to me as a child. For all the therapy *Annie* and I had done, I still saw this exploration of who I was as terrifying. I also need to forgive myself and forgive *The Girls*, for all the things we have done. The way my system moulded itself into a type of robotic machine, responding to circumstances with an intuitive and necessary lack of moral compass, ensuring our survival. Things this body, my system, did would make the skin of an innocent writhe. Or, even worse, elicit pity. Pity seems the worst of all. It denotes a sense of less than adequate; something is unacceptable, even unchangeable. Perhaps pathetic.

The shame and self-loathing all make sense when I look at my life through this lens. Understanding, even having compassion for the Parents, peels away layers of anger, hiding self-hatred, making room for me to forgive myself. Only those who have survived childhood trauma can truly understand this without revulsion. It is the locked closet in each of our lives. The humiliation we hide away, pretending to the world, and even our intimate friends, that we are fine. More often than I care to admit, I choose to live with my dark secrets. It feels safer than forgiving myself, and fuels the need to keep our shame and disgrace hidden. Would self-forgiveness be the key unlocking the door hiding my shame? Would it clean out my dark closet? Allow me to breathe freely?

The enormity of this task, of forgiving myself for what I did to survive, feels much harder than letting go of unresolved desires and expectations around the Parents. The Parents were dead, and I lived halfway around the world from reminders of them. Everything with them was already set in stone. There was no do-over, no opportunity for them to show remorse for their actions (another fantasy still invading my thoughts and dreams). They were gone. This task would be entirely mine to manage.

Forgiveness is a loaded question, and one I will wrestle with for the rest of my life. To forgive myself and to help *The Girls* respond from a healthier place, I have to find a way to move beyond the Parents and the ramifications of our history on my life today. Therapy assures me there is no easy way around this. Triggers, relationship issues and frustrations will forever be with me.

What if instead of denying these issues, I could honour their place in my/our lives? Respect their importance because they are part of our history. *The Girls*—and I—could learn to lean into the gentle grace and mercy coming from forgiveness. I'm no saint and have no quick answers. Time will tell is trite, but a very apt response in this circumstance.

Grief's Journey

For everything I have lost, I have gained more; my existence balanced delicately on a set of scales. On one side, hope and a future, on the other, grief and loss. My scale gently tips toward grief, not enough to upset the balance, but enough to be a noticeable theme in my life. I refuse to dwell on this. Instead, I acknowledge the place it holds. It is not a dark place, more of a placeholder where emotions collide and where in losing, I am gaining. By letting go, I am receiving. I choose to believe we all do this—hold our emotions and experiences in some sort of balance. It is the nature of life.

Each Mother's Day, I consider this careful balance. I mourn the loss of a mother/daughter relationship I will never have, while my own heart overflows with joy, pride and amazement at the gift of raising these three amazing humans who are my children. Balancing the grief I experience with everything my children give me.

My children hold grief in their own lives, the obvious being the loss of their birth mother. We don't really discuss it much these days. On the odd occasion, conversations ensue, but those are more about culture. I suspect the loss of their birth mother is held deep in their hearts, and perhaps not seen as relevant in their lives at the moment. I think culture is a bigger theme for them, holding in balance what an amazing country the Philippines is, their country of origin, and acknowledging the poverty they came from, while appreciating all the benefits and security they have living in a Western culture.

For the kids, there is also the lurking grief of losing Tom and me. It is something DoCS instilled in us in the application process—our children would feel this fear after having lost their birth mothers. Perhaps I've been fortunate; I haven't seen this acutely in our kids' lives (I have seen this demonstrably with other families who have children with significant attachment issues). The need for attachment was more evident when they were younger, always asking questions and wanting to know more. As young adults, they were developing their own perspectives and lives. I would like to think of this as a testament to their growth and adaptation.

I think about our children's birth mothers. My heart cannot comprehend their grief in the choice to give up their child. It seems unfathomable for them to place their child in the arms of a stranger whose job it was to decide their baby's future. In the Philippines, when giving up their baby, birth mothers are required to sign a *Voluntary Deed of Relinquishment*. It's a flimsy piece of paper giving the authorities the right to determine what's best for their child.

Their birth mothers had to hold in balance the knowledge they couldn't provide for their child and, on the other side, love—a pure, unadulterated mother's love wanting to always hold their child close. They walked into the government office (or orphanage), arms full of love, and left empty, holding only grief.

Did my mother experience grief? I am sure Mother felt this deeply over the children she miscarried. I want to ask a different question. If she were here, I would ask if she felt grief when Father took me to their bedroom. Did she turn a blind eye, have a drink and dive into her artistic world, painting, oblivious to what was happening at the other end of the house?

What about when I went on 'outings' with Father's friends? Did she dissociate herself, removing me from her life enough not to care, or was there some seed of grief over not speaking up, or trying to protect me? I want to believe there was grief. Honestly? I doubt it. But admit she was probably numb. No grief, no loss, no pain. Maybe there was initially, but her whole desire focused on Father. She would have minimised, even negated, any responsibility she felt toward me. I suspect she walked through much of her life this way, protecting herself from feeling grief over what was happening to me. I want to find a small sense of hope, but I know this is my child's heart speaking. Pragmatically, I can't imagine she grieved.

In my kaleidoscopic existence, grief seems to sit front and centre. Because of *The Girls*, grief enters my life unexpectedly. A small trigger and I'm suddenly swimming neck-deep in a torrent of emotion. I see a mum hugging her child and realise, with a tinge of sadness, I was never hugged by Mother. None of those deep, long held, squeeze me like a teddy bear until my stuffing comes out hugs I dreamed would envelop me in a sense of safety and love.

I dream of the day my children marry and of who their amazing partners might be. My parents were not at my wedding. I had no father to walk me down the aisle, or mother to fuss over me and help me get dressed for my big day.

I have spent hours daydreaming about what a healthy relationship with Mother would have looked like. I have nothing to compare it to apart from idyllic movies, which I know are not an accurate representation of life. So, instead, I sit with emptiness.

In examining the role of grief in my life, I have to acknowledge *Annie*. She lived a significant part of my life and experienced more than her fair share of loss.

Annie owns the grief of not birthing her own children. *Annie*'s history is laced with the trauma and guilt of forced abortions and circumstances leaving her (us) unable to have children biologically. I know she feels this grief acutely, not having partaken in the mystical process of childbirth.

She and I share the grief of not having a mother. For *Annie*, time and stillness have made her firmly stoic and pragmatic about the loss. When my brother called and let me know Mother had died, there was a stab of grief. It felt foreign to me. *Annie* instead, was relieved. It was a chapter in our history she could shut the door on.

Annie still feels a profound sense of loss and grief over the Philippines. She was the one who travelled and spent time there. While adoption was her dream, she also wanted to live amongst the nationals, her days spent in quiet anonymity amongst the Filipino people. This was an unrealistic fairytale dream, but still something she yearned for and lost.

If I think about this holding of grief as a set of scales, it takes a counterbalance. For every moment of sadness and loss, I also hold hope. I didn't have parents at my wedding—but I will be at my children's celebrations. I never knew the tenderness of a cuddle, but

I give these to my children at every opportunity. Young adult boys are not so keen on a bear hug from their mother, so these days, my hugs are verbal affirmations of their lives, but they are still a valuable counterbalance to what I lost.

What surprised me, but in the end makes complete sense, is how over the course of the past few chapters I've been looking at the anger in my life, which then moved into forgiveness, and here I am smack in the middle of a chapter on grief. My therapist would be proud of my ability to acknowledge this. Forgiveness follows anger, then mingles with grief; this is a hopeful, healing process.

Anger, for me, is about the injustice of what happened to all of us. It wasn't fair; it wasn't right, and it robbed us of a childhood full of joy. It is not fair for *Angry Woman* to carry the ongoing hatred of Mother and all she represents. Or the horrific task of holding all the anger (and subsequent pain) for the rest of *The Girls*. I want them desperately to hear how I appreciate all they did. Maybe those words can be a counterweight in their scale of grief and healing.

Forgiveness is a word fraught with challenges and misunderstandings. Maybe pity is better. Can I pity the Parents? Helping me to let go? My version of forgiveness. Just as important, can I forgive myself? Can I accept my learned behaviours were not of my doing but things instilled, learnt, as a means of survival?

I am still coming to terms with grief, understanding I have not arrived. But at least I am aware. From time to time, I ponder whether grief might really be a beautiful thing, something to be treasured, not feared. Could grief then be the holding place I alluded to? Or is it more? A sacred spot where memories of love lost and love wished for knit together and create their own kind of joy?

Defining Success

My children are now grown, and I watch as they fly into adulthood with all its fractious beauty, unafraid. I still marvel at our journey. Being entrusted to care for their souls, and how they've become such extraordinary humans. Like many mothers, I wonder what I have done to deserve the honour of motherhood, the gift of being their parent. I'm standing in the doorway, waving each of them off as they begin their own journeys of self-discovery, confident they are ready to explore their futures.

It begs the question, have I done a good job? Parented each of them well? Have I given them every opportunity to grow and understand their own hearts? Is there a litmus test I can apply to prove I've been a good parent?

Recently, in the midst of a heated discussion with one of my kids, they declared emphatically and with colourful language, 'Mum, you are wrong!' I don't remember what the conversation was about, but I know I felt firmly put in my place, summarily reprimanded and dismissed as they turned and walked away. Stunned, I stood quietly, trying to determine my next words. This irritation gradually changed to a quiet smile. This—*this*—was my barometer for success. I knew I'd grown my children well because they had a mind of their own, they didn't need to agree with me, and they felt safe doing so. Confused? Hear me out.

Growing up, *Annie*'s life revolved around rules. Internally, rules to keep our system safe, alive. For *The Girls*, it was all about obedience. Do what the Parents or abuser said and maybe it wouldn't hurt so much. Externally, it was rules to make the Parents happy. *Annie* was desperate for their love. So, when she was told to get something from the kitchen for Mother, she obeyed without question. When told to do the dishes or take out the trash, she simply did it. It was perfunctory obedience at best; *Annie* knew it would make little difference. And when she failed, as she knew she would, they punished her, and she knew she deserved it, taking the chastisement obediently, in a futile hope to earn their love. Always hopeful.

As Tom and I were going through the adoption process, DoCS drilled into us that adopted children of any age come with the challenges of grief, loss and abandonment. My children lost their first family, so they would live with the fear they might lose us. It was my job as an adoptive parent to mitigate their fear as much as I could. Being a place of safety for them, helping manage and process those emotions as they grew. No matter what we did, this painful history would always remain an underlying theme in their lives. Always. Even after all these years, I can still see this loss in each of them. Especially in how they relate to me. Sometimes a push-me-pull-you relationship, desperate for my approval, but just as determined to be independent. It's as if this visceral loss of their birth mother is always with them.

This loss of a mother is something that bonds me with my children. It lingers in my heart, a quiet murmur, where I question: would my life have been different if Mother had been able to care for me?

From time to time, at events for my children, I stand with other parents as we barrack and cheer our kids on. I've been surprised when parents have leaned over and said in amazement that how their kids have turned out had nothing to do with them. A half-laughing, self-deprecating reflection on their own failings.

Instead, I would dare to hope I've had something more than a minor role to play in this wonderful journey to normalcy. Danny, our youngest, graduated from high school this year. As he walked through a supportive crowd forming their school's traditional guard of honour at the Year 12 students' farewell assembly—parents, grandparents, siblings and students—I was in awe. He shook hands with well-wishers as he made his way through the makeshift human tunnel. I watched with great pride, realising the amazing young man he was becoming. He's not perfect; at 18, he shouldn't be. What I saw before me was a young man with the heart, the mind and the knowledge to step into the world, knowing he could tackle any of the storms that life would surely throw his way.

My heart was full knowing I played some part in who he had become.

These days, my young adult kids like to remind me they know more than I do. I am a technology Neanderthal as far as they are concerned (admittedly they are right). I am out of step with today's trends, whether in music, fashion or the subtle nuances of online communication. I'm quite confident they deliberately mumble just to ensure I don't hear something, and then they pronounce me deaf, refusing to repeat their query, as if I'm a bother. This is one of their favourite, slightly humiliating, control mechanisms with me. But it makes me giggle nonetheless, it's simply another form of bonding.

And of course, there are the real arguments, when I have offended their young adult sensibilities or curtailed their desire for freedom in some obscure way. The best is the unexplained, 'Mum, you just don't get it!' After which, they storm off or hang up the phone to emphasise their point.

All of this irritates the crap out of me. But it also makes me smile. It means one simple thing—they are confident, not just in themselves, but in my love for each of them. Arguments abound; deriding comments ensue. But in the end, they do this because they are confident of my love, certain and secure in my affection for each of them.

My love for my children is not something they can win or lose. It is not performance-based like my life growing up. It simply is. I love them, no matter what. In seeing their growing independence, I know they have an innate understanding of my love for them. This sense of security was something *Annie*, *The Girls*, and I never knew. The knowledge that my kids are living their fullest lives and pursuing their dreams has become the salve to my fractured heart.

Acknowledgements

Writing is a solitary occupation. I spend hours every day with ideas and concepts that are not only a creative expression of my soul, but something I hope, with careful crafting, will resonate with my readers. The perspective, the drive to write something meaningful, none of this could be done without the supportive writing community that is my pond. There are those I've known well for years now, doing zoom sessions or going on writing retreats. I would not be the writer I am today without their fabulous support. You know who you are, and my appreciation and love for you holds no bounds.

It is my privilege to have access to the fine teaching and support of Byron Writers Festival. A vibrant community of creatives that provide teaching and workshops that have been my inspiration for numerous years now.

Mentors continue to inspire and nurture my craft. Lee Kofman and Sarah Armstrong to name but a few. Their wisdom, critique and care continue to inspire me.

There are memoirists who have had a significant influence on my writing and commitment to writing true life experience. Al Close,

Sarah Martin and Mary Garden, your wisdom and insight are a delight to my heart.

Anna Featherstone, you opened my eyes to the fun and satisfaction of indie publishing. Your continued support always challenges me to be the best I can, embracing the joy of this writing journey. You never fail to encourage me to continue to try harder and give my work 110% of my effort.

For my friends in the adoption community. We come and go in each other's lives, but no matter when and where we catch up, we know that we get it. This journey, this craving for family that has made us friends. Thank you, always, for your love and support.

My nephew Andrew, thank you for being a slice of family to me, and for access to such important relics of our family history. It has put so much into perspective and helped to paint a more complete perspective of who Mother and Father were. I am grateful we found each other ... again!

My church community. They have embraced my foibled self, encouraging me to keep my eyes focused and my heart strong in God, as I embrace this creative gift of writing He has blessed me with.

And then there is of course, my immediate family. Thank you to my husband, who was such a calming support during the adoption process. Without him, we wouldn't have our amazing children, and for that I will always be grateful.

And finally, my three gorgeous young adult kids (because they will always be kids in my eyes), forever in my heart, and always an inspiration. I love you so much.

About Maggie ...

Maggie is an award-winning author whose memoirs *SPLIT* and *Fractured Motherhood* explore trauma, dissociation, adoption and the long arc of healing. Her work blends raw honesty with lyrical craft, illuminating how the past echoes through identity, family, and love.

Author Talks and Workshops

Maggie speaks widely on the topic of complex trauma and healing, using her story to reduce stigmas and change the narrative around mental health. Sharing her story in a relaxed, informative and fun way, engaging audiences of all sizes. She is available to share her story at libraries, festivals, and conferences.

Her writing workshops are a balance between group discussion and practical exercises. She teaches on a variety of topics and can also cater to your groups specific needs.

For More Information:

www.maggie-walters.com | maggie@maggie-walters.com

Rehoboth Sampaloc Ministries

Rehoboth Sampaloc Ministries (RSM) is in the mountains east of Manila in the province of Rizal. It is a place of care and belonging—offering education and medical support not only to the children who live there, but to the surrounding community as well. For our children, RSM was home. It was where they were held in safety and steadiness until they could be with us. We carry enduring gratitude for the love and dedication that shaped their early lives and the work that continues there still.

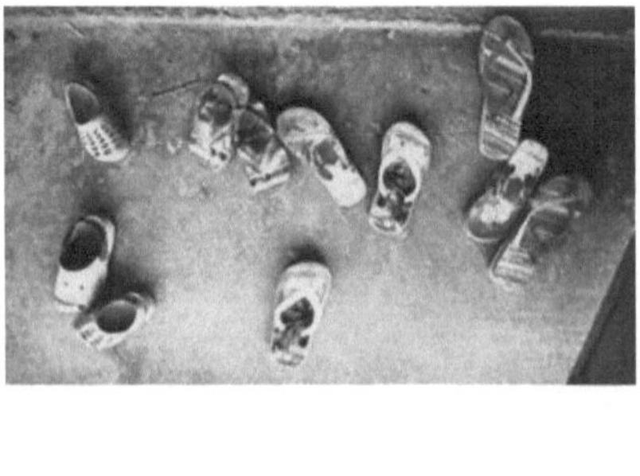

www.ingramcontent.com/pod-product-compliance
Lightning Source LLC
LaVergne TN
LVHW041623060526
838200LV00040B/1409
9780648603832